"I'm so excited that my friend Drenda has written this book! Anyone with a family knows how challenging it can be, and Drenda brings such a fun and fresh perspective on how to do life with family well. I can't wait to see the impact *The New Vintage Family* has on many families!"

LISA BEVERE, MESSENGER INTERNATIONAL AND BEST-SELLING AUTHOR

"Drenda Keesee has written a book that will bless families. The Keesee family is precious to me. They have trained their children to be godly and loving, and that's the way our families should be. You will be blessed by reading it."

DODIE OSTEEN, COFOUNDER OF LAKEWOOD CHURCH

"I've been all over the world and preached for many people, but I find that Gary and Drenda are two of the most unique people I've ever met. If anybody can be considered 'family people,' these two definitely are. And if anyone can teach you how to have a successful family life, these two certainly can! They know how to minister the Word of God effectively, so instead of just confessing something, you actually possess it. I enjoy Gary and Drenda very much, and I know you will enjoy this book."

JESSE DUPLANTIS, AUTHOR, SPEAKER, AND FOUNDER OF JESSE DUPLANTIS MINISTRIES

"Gary and Drenda are amazing parents. The proof of this is seen in the way their children passionately love the Lord. Lisa and I are glad to call them friends. In *The New Vintage Family,* Drenda beautifully addresses the challenges of family life and provides a refreshing perspective on navigating it!"

JOHN BEVERE, MESSENGER INTERNATIONAL, AUTHOR, MINISTER

"After meeting and experiencing the dynamics of the Keesee family, I was totally inspired to model my family after theirs. As a mother of two small girls, I noticed the Keesees worked hard and played hard together. They made a point to always be interactive with their children, inspiring them to become the persons God created them to be! I am happy to say that today I have an amazing family that has fun together because I modeled my family after theirs by always pursuing God first, working together and playing together! I wouldn't have it any other way!"

ANGELIQUE GATES, HOMESCHOOL MOM

"It's such an honor to know the whole Keesee family. Jesus said, 'You will know them by their fruit,' and Gary and Drenda have demonstrated such good fruit in the lives of their own children. In the midst of a secular society that continually degrades what the family is all about, it's clear to see that the godly upbringing and standards by which they raised their children should be used as a shining light example for the whole world to see. The proof is in the pudding."

ANDREW IRONSIDE, HILLSONG LEADERSHIP COLLEGE LECTURER AND TRAINER

"You can tell a lot about a couple by looking at their family, and the Keesee family is a true testament to that. Not only do Gary and Drenda's children love to spend time with their parents, they are also heavily involved in their ministry—they don't just have fun together, they work together. Gary and Drenda exemplify what it means to value family, investing into their marriage and children. They have raised them to walk with the Lord and be leaders in their generation. Through their effective parenting, they have built a strong family model for their community. They are creating an incredible legacy, and we can truly learn a lot about family from this book."

TINA KONKIN, SPEAKER AND RELATIONSHIP COUNSELOR

"After many years of military service and law enforcement, Post-Traumatic Stress (PTSD) was tearing our marriage and family apart. We found restoration in the biblical teaching of Gary and Drenda on faith, family, and finances. Today we live a complete spiritual and financial life and are able to minister to other struggling families, showing them real evidence. This book is an amazing resource for marriage and family. Few authors come close to blending the biblical truths with the modern world the way Drenda does. Prepare to be renewed!"

ADRIENNE AND AARON WARD, RETIRED MILITARY AND CURRENT POLICE OFFICER

"I can't think of anyone better to write a book on parenting than Drenda Keesee. Having known Gary and Drenda along with their family for years, and having spent time with them in their home, the fruit of great parenting is clearly evident in their children. Their wealth of wisdom, discernment, and understanding, which comes from years of pastoring a great church, building a wonderful ministry, and establishing a successful business, flows over into their family, and I am richer for not only knowing them personally but all their great kids! This book will not only encourage parents, but give you the wisdom, discernment, and understanding on how to raise great kids, who not only live full and rich lives but will be a blessing to the world around them."

PETER J. MORTLOCK, SENIOR PASTOR, CITY IMPACT CHURCH, AUCKLAND, NEW ZEALAND

"Heaven on earth is a family business. I have known Gary and Drenda and their family for sixteen years. They have been forerunners in the area of family and have done family well. Their ministry has spanned into a global ministry encouraging others to do family God's way. Their book is timely and vital; read it and then let it change you!"

LEIF HETLAND, AUTHOR OF *SEEING THROUGH HEAVEN'S EYES*

"We all encounter people whom we see so much potential in, and then there are those who have the ability to bring out the best in others. Gary and Drenda are this kind of people. Each member of their family is unique, functioning in their own gifting and carrying the touch of God on their individual life. The strong relationships and family environment built over decades by this 'dad and mom' have created the family you see today. The greatest desire for any parent is that our children will outrun us. Gary and Drenda have made sure that all their children, and their families, will venture far beyond their present horizon to accomplish what some of us can't even dream of. Read and hear what they have to say."

PASTOR BEV MORTLOCK, B.A. MIN.

"Drenda is one of the most empathetic yet fun parents we know. She has the joy of the Lord on her even when family life does not look so joyful. This book contains keen insights from a mother who doesn't give up and prays through. You will learn about effective family ground rules that work."

MARY HUDSON, AUTHOR OF THE *JOYFUL PARENT=HAPPY HOME*

DRENDA KEESEE

THE NEW

Vintage
FAMILY

A VINTAGE LOOK FOR
THE MODERN-DAY FAMILY

Unless otherwise noted, all Scriptures are taken from the *Holy Bible, New International Version*. NIV®. Copyright © 1973, 1978, 1984 by International Bible Society. Used by permission of Zondervan Publishing House. All rights reserved.

Scriptures noted NKJV are from the *New King James Version*. Copyright © 1982 by Thomas Nelson, Inc. Used by permission. All rights reserved.

Scriptures noted ESV are taken from the *The Holy Bible, English Standard Version*®, copyright © 2001 by Crossway, a publishing ministry of Good News Publishers. Unauthorized reproduction of this publication is prohibited. All rights reserved.

Scriptures noted NLT are taken from the *Holy Bible*, New Living Translation, copyright © 1996, 2004, 2007 by Tyndale House Foundation. Used by permission of Tyndale House Publishers, Inc., Carol Stream, Illinois 60188. All rights reserved.

Scriptures noted MSG are from *The Message*. Copyright © 1993, 1994, 1995, 1996, 2000, 2001, 2002. Used by permission of NavPress Publishing Group.

Scriptures noted NET are from the *NET Bible*® copyright ©1996-2006 by Biblical Studies Press, L.L.C. http://netbible.com All rights reserved.

ISBN 978-1-94230-620-7

Published by Free Indeed Publishers
Distributed by Faith Life Now

Faith Life Now
P.O. Box 779
New Albany, OH 43054
1.888.391.LIFE

You can reach Faith Life Now Ministries on the Internet at www.faithlifenow.com

Literary development by Kirsten Keesee and interior design by Koechel Peterson & Associates, Inc., Minneapolis, Minnesota.

Printed in the U.S.A.

I WANT TO DEDICATE THIS WRITING TO OUR FAMILY, THE INSPIRATION FOR THIS BOOK

To Gary, my most faithful friend, godliest man I know, everything good in our life, and my cherished loving husband . . . still looking forward to spending the rest of my life with you in our growing love and family (and eating your delicious homemade waffles!). You have confirmed God's gifts are best!

And our five fold . . .

To Kirsten, "KJ", forever our baby daughter and "Jane Austen" of the family, sweet, composed, and gorgeous writer. You are the joy God promised! I appreciate your gracious literary labor to help me share these timeless truths that have given us the good (and busy) life! (And your personal challenges to bungee and parachute jump and to traverse Asian nations, dreams I probably wouldn't have done without your inspiration!)

To Amy, compassionate, artistic, thoughtful daughter. Motherhood has only enhanced your incredible beauty and pure, passionate voice to worship with the heartbeat of our God. You are the living image of these gracious truths. Thank you for the many rescues!

To Tim, tenderhearted, principled, and true. Son, you are wise beyond your years and will continue to amaze and advance as a minister, worshipper, and man. The call of God and your sense of justice and loyalty outshine the darkness.

To Tom, son, your creative energy and passionate brilliance not only inspire me to stay young; they call out the greatness in others. Your hero's heart to heal the broken shines brightly as you fight sinister forces and make sure good always wins!

To Polly, funny, whimsical, and yet wise, straightforward, and determined daughter. You are a stunning beauty, but there is even so much more beneath that sparkle, wit, and laughter, a genuine and huge-hearted life-giving friend and sweet mother.

And I love all our children "in-love" who gave us . . . (ta-da) the grandbabies, Journey, Dawson, Ivory, Cadence, and Donny, and the ones to come . . . you are the future. Love one another and live life for God. Grand-mama loves you, and you are grand indeed!

Contents

PART 1

The Modern Family

RECOGNIZING THE PROBLEM

Gary's Family, Thomas, Marjorie, Gary, Krista, Rhonda, and Dennis.

Drenda's Family, Donald, Polly, Drenda, and Donny.

Set the Stage

A POLAROID SNAPSHOT

The Sixties brought us bell-bottom jeans, a new genre of music linked to the British Invasion and Motown, and the advent of color TV, but behind the scenes a prolific amount of problems was stirring. In 1966, a *TIME* cover story actually asked, "Is God Dead?" The Sixties were a turning point for the standards of family and marriage, and one from which our culture still hasn't recovered. Prayer was taken out of the school system. Racial tension resulted in outbreaks of violence. Media drifted from family-focused entertainment, and new ideals on the family were birthed.

I was raised in the early '60s in a small town in Georgia, where a fifth-grade teacher introduced me to the propaganda of the feminist movement. I grabbed ahold of that teaching and turned into a marriage-hating, man-hating, family-hating broken young woman. Men hurt me at a young age, and I channeled that hurt toward the cause. I used feminism as an excuse for revenge on the people who had hurt me.

The mantra of the Sixties was to do what felt good and ignore the consequences. It may have started with intentions of love and harmony, but on its misplaced foundation, it grew from a movement to a rebellion. While people were losing themselves in the hype, the consequences mounted, and today they are boiling over into the lives of our children. More than fifty years after prayer was removed from public schools, we are reaping *major* repercussions from those decisions.

The family system has been flipped on its hinges, and we are facing a cultural war on marriage, resulting in unbelievable statistics of teen suicide, divorce, and domestic violence. Fewer couples are marrying and instead are just cohabiting. Many no longer feel there's anything wrong with living together before marriage, but the facts don't lie: "Cohabiting couples are more likely to split up. When they do, they often form new partnerships and have additional children, creating a complex web of half-siblings, stepparents, child support payments, and family visits."[1] Innocent children are the biggest losers of the family breakdown, but the parents lose, too.

People in general aren't investing in family anymore. The culture is pushing an antifamily agenda, attacking and rebranding what God created. Because a house divided cannot stand (Mark 3:25), Satan wants to get a hand in your family so he can stop you from accomplishing your destiny.

We are on the verge of another turning point in the culture. The birthing labors of the *new family* have started, and the media has an epidural on hand. The culture is in a pivotal season of decision between throwing the family model out altogether, or fighting to get back to ground zero . . . *the vintage family*, refashioned and repurposed, by reclaiming its origin.

My children grew up in a radically different era than mine, with instant access to information and entertainment via the Internet, with moral ethics being publicly challenged by our government and education system. Will marriage still be valued ten years from now? Will families still be honored? I believe in the principles of the vintage family, because I want to protect the future of all children, grandchildren, and great grandchildren. I want there to be peace and joy in family life again. I want to invade the culture that is trying to twist and dilute families, and I want to bring in the strongest, clearest form of the family system—the one that works.

Many are feeling an emptiness in the changes of our world, and they are longing for the "good old days." They want the loving Dick-Van-Dyke father at the door, home from work, saying, "Honey, I'm home!" They want the nurturing mother in her red-checkered apron and matching red lipstick who has dinner set on the table. And they want the whole household sitting around a table, exchanging stories over dinner. They want the vintage image because it was *simple.*

> The culture is in a pivotal season of decision between throwing the family model out altogether, or fighting to get back to ground zero . . . the vintage family, refashioned and repurposed, by reclaiming its origin.

The past has become a new craze with youth. Because many teenagers didn't grow up with a whole family or a value system, they are obsessed with eras that featured a strong family image. Fads such as thrifting, becoming a hipster, and even wearing vintage fashions have become popular. People want to know what it was like to live in simpler times. What is it like to shop in a little store? What is it like to eat an organic meal free of chemicals, pesticides, and fillers?

Parents who grew up watching black-and-white '50s TV Land shows that depict families working together want that for themselves. The problem is, to have this you have to embrace the principles that built the vintage family. They can't get the fruit without the seed. In the absence of principles, many fathers have abandoned their families, searching after their own pleasure. A disturbing number of moms, who were hardwired by God to care for and nurture their families, are abandoning their children emotionally and leaving them to care for themselves. And many families hardly communicate, let alone share a meal together.

We used to hear about "troubled teens," but now it's elementary and middle school children. Kids are growing up faster because they are exposed to adult problems younger and to pain they were never meant to bear. They are in turn doing things such as cutting themselves (revealing the pain they inwardly carry), struggling with eating disorders, rebelling and running away from their homes, denying their identity, and committing suicide. All of these troubles are not the real problem—they are symptoms of the root problem—*the breakdown of the family*.

Many parents want the best for their children; they just don't know how to give it to them. That's because nobody took the time to train them on how to parent. When it's all said and done, family is what matters the most—yet it is one of the areas many people are the least prepared for. There are processes and principles that set you up for greater success in parenting, and when you apply them, family life can be fun again! I want to take a look at the vintage model that made it work. What were the components of it? What was family life like? How can you achieve those same results in your modern family? This book is going to give you the dynamic tools you need to transform your family life and repurpose your family to receive God's best!

Finding "Normal"

THE PURSUIT TO REGAIN FAMILY LIFE

"Other things may change us,
but we start and end with the family."
ANTHONY BRANDT

My husband, Gary, and I love to spend our days off with home popped popcorn and whatever is playing on the Turner Classic Movie channel. One night we were watching the 1961 movie *Tammy Tell Me True*, and a scene came where Tammy went to babysit three little boys. Every nanny the rowdy boys had ever had quit, and when Tammy enters their house, she understands why. One boy is torturing an animal while his brother smokes a cigarette on the couch. The third little boy is running around the house screaming at the top of his lungs. When Tammy asks the parents, both college professors, why they let them act like that, their response is that they believe in allowing the children to explore their curiosity without boundaries.

After the parents leave, the boys try to sabotage Tammy into leaving. But Tammy is a strong Southern woman, and she starts enforcing order in the house, which is something the parents would detest. Once she has the boys calmed down, she begins to tell them about God. At first, they rattle on about their parents' belief that there is no God, but as Tammy tells them Bible stories, they start to lean in and listen carefully. By the end of the night, the little boys chime, "I hope you come back. You're the most interesting babysitter we've ever had." And one of them says, "Yes, I'd love to hear some more of those religious myths. We shan't tell our folks."

This classic movie was making fun of the idea of a family without rules and boundaries—but that's what the family model looks like today, and we see the outcome of that mirrored in society. Pop psychology from the Fifties and Sixties taught parents to introduce adult themes early and allow children to explore their curiosity, and we now have a generation that behaves as those children did.

Life was simpler before then. The future felt more secure and brighter than today. Marriages lasted. On Sundays, families went to church and spent the day together taking an afternoon drive or playing board games or baseball in the backyard. Families took picnics with buckets of chicken or made homemade ice cream while taking turns cranking the handle. Kids rode in cars with the windows down, stretched across the backseat on warm summer nights headed on road trip vacations. We watched TV together when there were only three stations to choose from, but it felt as though there was more worth watching.

You may be too young to remember any of this, but you've seen glimpses of it on TV Land reruns. There was a time when there was innocence in childhood. Marriages were expected to stay together until "death do us part." Men were expected to lead the family, provide security, work Monday to Friday, wash the car on Saturday, and take the family to church on Sunday. Somehow there was enough money on one income! Because men stayed committed to the family, it enabled moms to prioritize raising their children and taking care of family needs over wants that forced them to work away from family. But funny, they were more fulfilled. Life was simple and good for most. Were there problems? Sure. But not nearly to the degree we see today!

What changed? What went wrong? I asked some seventy- and eighty-year-old women, and one responded, "The biggest thing is that mothers left their children to go to work. I stayed home with my children, and it was the best time of my life." Another said, "Once my children started school, I worked a night shift, but I was home to get the kids off to school and home when they returned. They knew I was there." One woman said, "Men were leaders then. We were happier. Life was simpler. It was a better life than the stress I see my daughter living with today."

Women have more choices today but are statistically less happy than ever in recorded history. Could it be that the vintage values families of old possessed made the difference?

I asked women what we need to do to recapture the important things and more of what matters for our lives. Their answers . . .

> First, we must learn how to simplify and focus on what really matters. Second, we must understand how to build on the right foundation, with principles that work. We must build our families on timeless truths.

"We need more Christian men in leadership."

"Parents need to stop letting technology control their family."

"Before it's too late, mothers need to realize that while they can do many things, nothing is more important than their children."

"My daughter is divorced and so self-focused. I feel sorry for my grandson. He's never had any security. It's selfishness."

Is it possible to rediscover what used to make families work? Yes! Vintage is back. Retro is cool, and it works in our families, too.

First, we must learn how to *simplify and focus on what really matters.* Second, we must understand how to *build on the right foundation, with principles that work. We must build our families on timeless truths.*

The Light That Rises or the Unraveling of Our Culture?

So much dysfunction happens in families, hidden away in the secrecy of their homes. The effect of that dysfunction doesn't appear publicly until the children begin to act it out as they grow older. We are appalled by the shocking statistics of teen suicide, drug use, and pregnancy out of wedlock, but the root of those dysfunctional issues is planted early in young people's lives.

When parents are busy about their things and unwilling to make the necessary sacrifices for their family, their children adopt that mindset. The kids emulate what their parents do, and now we have a culture of entertainment-addicted children raised to seek their pleasure above anything else. The culture is in a dark place, and families can either be the light that rises or the very unraveling of our culture.

This became evident to me during a counseling session Gary and I had with a couple having marital issues. The wife was working three jobs and raising the two children, while the husband spent all of their money buying a boat, a sports car, and other major purchases. He acted as though he was God's gift to the world, a big shot with nothing to show for it besides mounds of debt and a devastated family.

In their counseling appointment, the wife pled, "I'm so weary! I am working all of these jobs and trying to take care of the family, and it's too much."

When Gary confronted the husband about his out-of-control spending and how his wife felt, he simply retorted, "Well, at least I'm not seeing another woman."

"Is that all your responsibility is in this marriage?" Gary asked, clearly frustrated with this man. "You think she should carry all of the finances, the kids, and the whole weight of everything while you're this little boy who pitches temper tantrums and does what he wants?"

The husband proceeded to push the blame onto his wife and justify himself. He was comfortable looking down on the world from his throne of debt. Pride made him deaf to wisdom, and he walked out with the same poisoned thoughts he brought into our session. My heart went out to the children when I considered the turmoil and hurt to which they were being subjected.

Gary and I own a financial services business that helps people get out of debt and invest securely. Years ago, Gary went on an appointment to a Christian home, where he sat down with the husband and wife to discuss their finances at a table facing their living room. He was shocked to see two small children in the living room watching television; but not just television—porn.

Gary assumed this couple must not know what the kids were watching, so he said, "Do you realize what is on your TV?"

The father glanced at his children and remarked nonchalantly, "They're going to learn about it eventually."

Gary was blown away with disgust. "Sorry, I'm not doing this appointment. I'm not going to watch this. If you let your children watch this, you're sending them down a road of destruction." And he left.

We have seen these types of dysfunctional situations in hundreds of families on appointments. I've watched so many parents who have given up hope of controlling their children and allow them to control the family instead. These situations are not anomalies. The truth is that the bar for families has reached a pivotally low point, but there is hope.

It's because of situations such as these that I have such a passion for families. It angers me when I see young girls trying to care for siblings so their mom can date an abusive boyfriend. And when that boyfriend is aggressive toward that young girl, the mom takes the boyfriend's side over the safety of her children because she is so desperate for love. This all too common scenario saddens my heart.

As parents, this is why we *should* be passionate about families. Stories such as that *should* upset us and make us rise up to protect families, because that is how God feels about His young children in these circumstances. God needs people to get frustrated with the current broken system so we declare, "Hey, there's a better way! We don't have to have this dysfunction here."

The Infinite Value of Children

Many Christians have swept the topic of family under the rug through the years. Somehow talking about "family" isn't spiritual. How do we think their Father God feels about what is happening to them? I believe that God is *very* into talking about family.

When parents brought their children to Jesus to pray for them, the disciples rebuked the parents. The disciples had the same mentality that many Christians have today, but Jesus said, "Let the little children come to me, and do not hinder them, *for the kingdom of heaven belongs to such as these*" (Matthew 19:14).

Jesus understood the value of those children—the value that many in our time have forgotten. Many significant figures in the Bible did their great acts as children or were enabled to do their great acts because their parents recognized the value of their lives and took precautions to protect them—Moses, David, Jeremiah, Josiah, and yes, even Jesus.

Children will rise to be our next leaders. That is why Jesus said, "For the kingdom of heaven belongs to such as these." He understood those children would become the next generation of disciples, apostles, and prophets. Jesus wasn't nearsighted!

Second Chronicles 34:1–3 describes the story of an incredible boy named Josiah:

> Josiah was eight years old when he became king, and he reigned in Jerusalem thirty-one years. He did what was right in the eyes of the LORD and *followed the ways of his father* David, not turning aside to the right or to the left. In the eighth year of his reign, while he was still young, he began to seek the God of his father David. In his twelfth year he began to purge Judah and Jerusalem of high places, Asherah poles and idols.

Eight years old, and yet he "followed the ways of his father David" and was excelling as the leader of Israel! By the time he was twenty years old, he was removing idols of other gods and purging Israel's cities of unrighteousness. The Bible says that there wasn't one king before Josiah who turned to God as he did, with all of his heart and strength in accordance with what God called right (2 Kings 23:25).

This is entirely in contrast to many of the youth we see today. Can you imagine an eight-year-old who is not only mature enough to be the President of the United States but to put God first in the country? We have a hard enough time trying to find *grown* men and women to do that! We have set the bar so low for people that we're just happy if they have a job. We have set the bar so low for children that we're satisfied if they stay in school and aren't on drugs. That might be where the modern family and culture have set the bar, but God has higher standards and greater plans for you and your family than barely above average.

I hate that Satan tries to come against families, because the family should be a safe place. Your family is where you should be able to be vulnerable and open; but instead, when Satan finds a place to enter, he takes advantage of the vulnerability God intended in our families and uses it to inflict deep wounds.

Have you ever been hurt by a family member or a loved one? Those wounds are deeper because you trusted them to look out for you. I've discovered that for many people their family is a source of pain and bitterness instead of healing and love. That is not how God designed it.

> "Don't you see that children are God's best gift?"
>
> PSALM 127:3 MSG

God designed the family unit to be a source of *protection* and *comfort*. When the family model is in place, it is a powerful force. When two or more come together in one common vision, they are not easily broken or suppressed (Ecclesiastes 4:12).

"Don't you see that children are GOD's best gift? The fruit of the womb His generous legacy? Like a warrior's fistful of arrows are the children of a vigorous youth. Oh, how blessed are you parents, with your quivers full of children! Your enemies don't stand a chance against you; you'll sweep them right off your doorstep" (Psalm 127:3–5 MSG).

The family is under attack. The devil wants to cause division in your household, steal your family time, and make you feel disconnected. You have to be prepared to fight for your family and guard against the attacks of the enemy. And you are called to bring other families with you. When you know the truth about God's divine plan in the family system, you are called to protect that.

Getting Back to the Basics

In the Forties and Fifties, families used to pack a picnic, jump in the car, and go for a drive. It wasn't about entertainment, something on a screen, or everyone sitting around the table on their smart phones without any talking or communication. Mentorship is the byproduct of communication.

Many of today's families operate like a boardinghouse. They occupy space in the same house, but they have no connection or unity. The family is meant to be more than providing free room and board. If your situation is like that, you're missing out on one of the greatest blessings God gives.

I want to give you the hope right now that God's power and grace are greater than your mistakes. It's never too late for a fresh start. It's never too late to make a difference in your current circumstances and the lives of your children, and also in the families around you.

I've gotten to know Connie through our ministry and met her four sweet children, but little did I know the road leading up to her beautiful family. Connie's past was marred with family dysfunction and pain. At the age of three, she overheard her mom threaten her dad that she would tell Connie she didn't really belong to him. Connie understood that something wasn't right in her life, even though her dad showed her love. Not long after a relative sexually molested her at the age of six, her parents got divorced, leaving her feeling responsible for their divorce.

Her mother turned to alcohol, and when her father remarried three short months later, he radically changed his behavior toward

Connie and her brother. She found out he was not her biological father, but that he adopted her when she was two. Her new stepmom and her father began to beat Connie and her brother until the day Connie's father told her she reminded him of her mother. He packed her stuff into trash bags and left her at her mom's presumed employer. But since she was no longer employed there, the employer had to locate Connie's mother, who lived in a very impoverished area of town. Connie practically raised herself from that point on. As she grew older, she started smoking pot, acting promiscuous, and lost her virginity at thirteen years of age.

Connie found God and started to transform her life. She wrote her father a letter that explained she had forgiven him and still loved him. When she delivered it, her father told her he had never loved her, but he would let her know if that ever changed. Connie stopped going to church after that, developed an addiction to drugs, tried committing suicide with pills and cocaine, and when she woke up alive, she drank bleach to finish it off. The hospital staff said that the only time they saw that amount of drugs in someone's system was in autopsies.

Connie survived, went to rehab, and gave up drugs, but life didn't get easier. She struggled through a divorce and began life as a single mom. She decided she was tired of being hurt by men and that she would use men instead; she just wanted to have "fun." In the midst of her "fun," she got pregnant with her second child. Devastated, she prayed she'd miscarry and considered getting an abortion. That was when Connie turned her life back to God, and everything began to change. She felt God leading her to allow a family to adopt her baby, and that He had a plan and a purpose for who the parents were going to be. When Connie heard the couple's name, she knew instantly that this was their baby. It was a smooth process, and Connie still has a great relationship with the adoptive parents today.

Connie continued to turn her life around, giving up her hate and bitterness toward men and trusting God to lead her and guide her steps as a parent. She didn't think she would ever remarry or have another child, but today Connie is happily married with four children. Despite her past circumstances, she has continued to grow her family and strengthen her walk with God, trusting God to show her how to be the mother figure she didn't have growing up. Connie says that all of the things she's had to overcome seem insignificant compared to all of the victories in her life now.

Connie says, "God has used my husband to show me that the past is the past, His grace is sufficient for all things, and that *all* things are made new in Him. If God can do this in my life, He can do it for anyone! It doesn't take long for your life to change."

Courage comes when we know our Maker, our identity in His love, and what we possess in Him. No matter what has happened in your past, God has made a way for you, and you are redeemed through Him. If you've gone through a divorce, there's still a future for your family. Your past doesn't condemn your future, and God can heal the wounds from that situation in your family.

The future of your children is not determined by how your parents raised you. You don't have to make the same mistakes they did. If your parents divorced, it doesn't mean you have to get a divorce. If you didn't have parents who modeled success in marriage or parenting, you can still have success in your marriage and family. God will give you the grace and the instruction. God's grace is enough for you.

A Closer Look

A friend was in a jewelry store when he overheard a couple talking to the sales clerk. The young lady noticed a necklace with a pendant hanging on it in the glass encasing. The pendant was a cross, and there was a figurine man hanging on the cross. "That's strange," she said. "Who is the little man on that cross?"

Many Christians think that everyone has heard of Jesus Christ, but that's not true. Only twenty percent of American families attend church on any given week in the United States. *Twenty percent.* So where are these families learning about life? Where are these children learning to know right from wrong? If they aren't learning from God, you can be sure they are being taught *something* somewhere.

I've discovered that many parents do not even know what is happening in their own home. Their children are being attacked with unbelievable amounts of perverse images and ideas. So few parents are aware of the Internet content being fed to their children or what their children are exposed to when they hang out with friends. A video game might be rated for a couple of curse words in it, but when a child plays that level over and over, those "few" curse words multiply into an entire vocabulary.

> Who, or what, is really training your child? Who are you allowing to tell your children what life is all about?

I can't begin to explore all that technology has made available, but I'll give you one snapshot. One of the *Grand Theft Auto* video games was originally banned in Australia for containing extreme graphic violence and sexual content, but that game grossed $300 million in the United States.[2] So what does that say about our culture? Another of the *Grand Theft Auto* games contains a torture scene where the player chooses the method of torture to inflict (electrocution, water boarding, removing teeth, or beating with a heavy wrench) to extract information from a person. After choosing the type of torture, the player has to execute the torture on the victim. This game series also allows the player to explicitly rape and kill innocent women and rewards them with pornography throughout the game. That game has broken seven world records since its release in 2013, including best-selling video game and fastest video game to gross $1 billion.[3] The worst part is, although the game is rated "M" for mature, the game series is popular with children as young as *nine* years old.

We live in a tsunami of media persuasion and perversion. It's like a giant wave that is smashing against the younger generations beyond their ability to cope and steady themselves.

- Eleven years old is the average age of a child's first exposure to Internet porn.[4]
- The average American child will have seen 200,000 acts of violence and 16,000 murders on television by the age of 18.[5]
- The average American child between the ages of 2–17 spends 19 hours and 40 minutes watching TV a week.[6]
- The average parent only spends 38 minutes a week in meaningful conversation with their child.[7]
- 70% of television shows include sexual content, averaging about 5 sex scenes per hour.[8]

So let me ask you who, or *what,* is really training your child? Who are you allowing to tell your children what life is all about? Are they being taught right or wrong?

My intention is not to condemn anyone or to paint a picture of a crumbling culture that can't change. My point is that we need change, desperately, and change can only happen when enough people realize that we need it and are willing to stand for it. The problems in the family system are more than skin deep—they are a reflection of where the culture is as a whole. And whether you're experiencing these issues in your family or not, none of us can turn a blind eye to the new level of corruption trying to invade the nation.

The good news is that God has given us the ability to overcome. Our children don't have to fall prey to the traps of the enemy. "For I am the LORD your God who takes hold of your right hand and says to you, do not fear; I will help you" (Isaiah 41:13). God is on your side, and you don't have to go into this battle alone. As we move forward, pray that God helps you see what areas you need to focus on changing. Let the principles sink in and effect real change in you, your family, and the culture around you—because we are living in perilous times that call for change.

Have you noticed a negative image toward family increasing in popularity?

....

....

....

....

....

What is the greatest thing you want to take away from this book?

....

....

....

....

....

....

In what areas in your family would you like to see growth and change?

....

....

....

....

....

In what areas in your family are you pleased with and thankful for?

....

....

....

....

....

....

Tom's
⟫∙ MONOGRAPH ∙⟪

MY THIRD BORN

"Tom, get away from the edge!" I remember my father's words as though they were yesterday. His face was tense with stress, his grip firm on my arm.

In front of me lay a vast panorama filled with rolling mountains peppered with tall sky-stretching trees. The only thing between that invoking view and me was a sharp three-hundred-foot plummet to the bottom—the reason my father was sweating on this cool Colorado morning.

It was day six of our Keesee family vacation that consisted of our family renting an RV and blitzing through the West like a bandit on the run. It was not a normal family vacation, but our family was anything but average. We homeschooled, ran our own company, and pastored a church. My parents actually cared about each other, and we kids really got along, most of the time. Looking back on those days, I have to wonder how my parents stayed sane. I certainly didn't help to make their life less hectic or stressful. Then again, an RV trip across America with five kids bouncing off the walls wasn't a great help either.

Our family of seven had spent the better part of an hour making the trek, each of us alerted to the hopelessness of the climb by the continuous rain of complaints fired off by my younger sister Polly. With each melodic "I hate hiking!" I became more determined that I was better than the average human. I would run ahead and prove that this was nothing to me. If I was lucky, my speed and prowess would challenge my older brother, Tim, to an unspoken race to the top. Like many other days, my attempts were to no avail. He gated with consistent strides, his face more than annoyed by the teasing of his kid brother.

My mother was somewhere in the center of the group, talking about how awesome it was that we were all finally on our trip across America and making us all slow down to take family pictures in front of every rock and tree (if you think I'm joking, just ask my siblings). My father had the task of carrying the littlest of the clan, Kirsten. She was rather partial to riding on her daddy's shoulders and letting us all know that she was living the good life, broadcasting her smug expression atop her kingly tower.

That left my oldest sister, Amy, who didn't stray far from the adults. This was not because she was afraid. It was simply because she was born an adult, or so I had surmised during my summers of detective work. She enjoyed conversing with Mom and Dad about church and the complexities of going to college at an age much younger than pretty much anyone else had ever gone. She was the reason much of my adolescent life was spent getting in trouble. I could swear that I had seen her and my mother "Vulcan mind meld" (pardon my Star Trek reference). Amy could always tell if I had done any wrong, was doing wrong, or planned on doing wrong in the near future. The bottom line? My older sister helped to guard us convicts when Mom and Dad were busy with their priestly duties. This may be a great time to let you know that I tease about my family as a means of protecting my super sensitive and boyish heart. It's true . . . I would do absolutely anything for them. Just don't let them know I'm such a softy.

My role in the family was simple, really. I had the task of ensuring that life was never boring or simple for the other siblings or Mom and Dad. If there was danger, I found it. If there was something to be conquered, I was Napoleon. If everyone was too silent, I stirred up some chaos. I wasn't trying to be rebellious. I was just so darn curious and handsome.

I should have seen the signs that there was no place on the mountain for curiosity that day. There weren't many cats in the Colorado Rockies—let me put it that way. There was a plethora of danger hiding around every bend, and my dad was getting tired of being a cat herder.

"Tom, I said stay away from the edge!"

"I'm not even that close."

"It just takes one slip."

I was like every other full-blooded American middle child. I knew precisely what I was doing. I was fifteen after all, which might as well have been fifty when my accrued knowledge of everything the world had to offer was taken into account. I could stand close to the edge of danger and walk away unscathed with the best of them. Besides, leaning over the edge was the only way I could catch a glimpse of the rocks that I was throwing down upon unsuspecting wildlife below. There my father was, guarding his young ward from sudden death as a true father should. There I was, the young gallivanting youth who needed to assert his fearlessness at the edge of every mountain in Colorado; Lumberjack Batman and skater Robin.

It would have been fine if this were the first time that I heard those firm and commanding words, but it wasn't. My father pulled me away.

I've always been one to push the boundaries of what was both safe and humanly possible. I was born with a disease that many young men are born with . . . it's called stupidity. Every now and again, I just do dumb things. Those of you who are parents of boys are either laughing or crying by now. This is because you have man-children. Boys are not intentionally dumb; they just are, without even trying. Throwing firecrackers out of house windows, jumping motorcycles into trees, running on ice—all symptoms of stupidity. Don't worry, though, your child can get healing. There's a wonderful thing that fixes this illness. It's a little thing called *discipline.*

> Don't let your parenting become religious. Don't keep the amazing panorama of life from your children. Don't keep them from reaching for their dreams because you're afraid of the edge. Instead, be right there with them.

That morning I was particularly dumb. I don't think I had an ounce of sense in my lanky body. If I fell from that ledge, there was no breaking my descent. I would be met with the choice of either rocks or the tops of evergreen Yosemite pines—both were sure to be fatal to a mortal. If I did survive, the forest creatures would exact their vengeance on my rock-tossing terrorist hindquarters. Now that I've experienced much more discipline, I realize how foolish I was. I'd love to say that was the only time I did something foolish. I've had scores of learning opportunities that life has dealt me by way of my decisions. The only thing I can tell you is that my family is the reason I'm not a monument.

I thank God for my family every day and for my amazing parents. I could write a library of books about their heroism in the face of danger and still not encompass their outlandish deeds. My father is a true hero to me and will forever be that way no matter his age or strength. My mother will always be among the most beautiful women whom I've ever seen, because that is who my father told me she was every day I was raised. These ideals and words are not written in textbooks and can't be learned from Rosetta Stone in thirty days or less. They are instilled in your child from the day they are born to the day they march into the world.

The thing is, there's a danger that is always calling your children closer to the edge. They may think they know best. They may be curious or just lack some discipline. This is why you are the parent. The day my father grabbed my arm wasn't about him trying to shove his life values on me or to keep me from having fun. It was to protect me from myself. My father has since "grabbed my arm" on more than one occasion, which I am more than grateful for. But even more important than those moments of protection is the learning of how to follow the voice of our heavenly Father when He says, "Don't get too close to the edge."

"But I'm not even that close, God."

"It just takes one slip."

You see, going to the top of the mountain isn't wrong to do. How else can you see and experience many of the great things that life has? Don't let your parenting become religious. Don't keep the amazing panorama of life from your children. Don't keep them from reaching for their dreams because you're afraid of the edge. Instead, be right there with them. Guide them. Show them that God wants them to live a life full of adventure. But keep a watchful eye. What are your kids watching and playing? With whom are they spending time? Are you journeying with them or have you stopped somewhere down the hill? They need you in their life. And don't allow yourself to lose hope for that one in your family who may go too close to the edge by nature. He or she just may be made with that fearlessness because they are going to pull others away from the edge. Instead, keep ahold of their arm, spiritually. Some kids are going to take a bit more prayer and a bit more work. But you know, those kids just might be the ones who keep everyone's lives interesting and adventurous in the long run.

Drenda and
Tom 1988.

Celebrating Gary's 60th birthday in Hawaii.

One of our many cross-country road trips visiting Dead Horse Point. (Back left to right: Kirsten, Amy, Tim, Drenda, and Gary. Front left to right: Polly and Tom.)

Make a Statement

GETTING YOUR FAMILY TO THEIR DESTINY

"What can you do to promote world peace?
Go home and love your family."

MOTHER TERESA

Someone walked up to my husband and me once and said, "You know, you have to be the wealthiest people in the world." Gary smiled. "Why's that?"

"Because of your family," he said.

And it's true; there is nothing worth more than my family. It doesn't matter what happens in the world, I always know my family is there for me. I know that I can go home and get refueled spending time with my family. That is a great feeling.

Everyone starts life with dreams and visions. As children, we play games of success and winning rather than divorce court or bankruptcy. We want our lives to make a statement, to leave an impression. So what happens to change the exhilarating picture of success into a sea of sorrows and lost ambitions? For many, entering family life unprepared for bills, business, taxes, children, and all the negative pressure beats the living daylights out of the dreams and destiny locked deep within them by their Creator.

And instead of the family becoming the great joy it was intended to be, it's often seen as the blame for shattered dreams.

Several years ago when Gary and I were first coming out of our hopeless situation, Gary had a dream in which he was walking along the rock siding of a mountain when he heard people talking behind the rock. Then he was given a vision to see inside the mountain into a sealed cave, which had no entrance or exit. It was pitch black, except for the light of a small black-and-white TV casting pale shadows on the stone floor. Around it sat a small family that looked on distantly. Their eyes had dark circles under them, and their faces were gaunt. They were skin and bone. They were trapped in their situation.

> There is no greater reward in this life than having your family together, loving one another, and serving God.

Gary wanted to help them out of their rock-encased lifestyle, so he began to yell as loud as he could to catch their attention. They finally called back to him, but their voices were limp and lifeless.

"You have to get out of there!" he cried.

"But we can't get out. There's no door."

"You have to praise God," he said. "Turn to the Lord and begin to praise Him."

They began to praise God, but nothing happened.

"You need to praise Him with all of your strength!" he yelled.

As the family stood up and began to radically praise God, the rocks started to crumble and fall down, and the family came running out of the cave, rejoicing in God. They were rubbing their eyes and seeing light for the first time. There was a world of endless possibilities ahead of them.

I've discovered that most people live like that family in the cave. They live inside of a bubble, trying to survive, and just getting through life. They don't have any vision. They are surviving, but they aren't thriving. They feel trapped in their situation.

You are not destined to live in dark caves. You can enjoy the fresh air and fields, the mountains, and the endless possibilities God has made available for you. Your family is destined to be free and happy. Yes, God wants your family to enjoy life. "He gives us richly all things to enjoy" (1 Timothy 6:17 NKJV).

We have access to the Kingdom of God. We have access to a great future. The problem is many people don't know how to break out of that stronghold. Satan tries to encase us in survival mode, but there's an escape for your family. Your family can enjoy the benefits of God's Kingdom!

The Word of God promises the wisdom and insight to live a different existence than the average Joe, but you still have to walk it out. Not only is your family part of helping you reach your destiny, it is your reason, your "why"!

God strategically set up your family with the elements it needs to equip you for your destiny. If God could choose where to place you, and who to surround you with, don't you think He would choose those people strategically? Don't you think there is something those people are designed to bring to your life, and something you're designed to bring to theirs?

Your family is the anchor that keeps you grounded, connected, and accountable to something. It is designed to instill a vision of God's love and purpose in you from a young age. If your family growing up wasn't like that, you need to commit to making a change with your own children. You're not your parents nor are you bound by their mistakes.

Can you imagine if God placed us on the earth without any family? How would we even know how to begin to take care of ourselves? We would either disconnect from people altogether, or we would push ourselves into dangerous relationships to fill that void and end up getting hurt. We would resent God. Children who grew up with parents who aren't present in their lives act out like this.

People make mistakes. Families make mistakes. When a family is not partnered with God, the positive impact of family life is reversed and your family can equip you for your demise. Some family situations are so dysfunctional they are actually more detrimental to a child, but that's not how God intended it.

There's a price to pay to raise a healthy family. It costs money, time, and attention. But it's worth it! There is no career or accomplishment that I have loved as much as being a wife and mom. There is no greater reward in this life than having your family together, loving one another, and serving God.

It takes faith and courage, but you're equipped and called by God to lead your family down the road to a place of destiny. You are not as those who just hope, or as those who are destined to fail, but you are equipped by God to win.

It's time to agree with what your Father God says in His Word and no longer put up with a lifestyle of just getting by. There's no future when you're surviving. You can only see the end of the day, striving just to make it week to week, living paycheck to paycheck, and you can't get a vision for your destiny that way. God's people are called to live an exceptional life, so it's time to lift your head up above the chaos of every day and look at what could be.

When our family was broke (in multiple ways), we couldn't see a future. We could hardly see the end of the day through all of our problems. When you don't have a future financially, it's hard to have a future as a family, because everything your family needs takes money. Well, almost everything. We were oppressed by our situation. We didn't think there was any use in planning, because we had no money, no hope, and no answers.

Was that God's plan for our life? No! As soon as we realized that, we started down the path to a drastic life change. We woke up and understood that God always had a plan for our life and family. God has a plan for yours, too!

So how do you walk in that plan? How do you overcome your situation and the strongholds around you and walk in your family's destiny?

Step #1: Wake Up from Survival Mode

On January 18, 1982, four Thunderbird aircrafts were practicing for an air show. In their routine, all four planes flew in a diamond pattern, with one leading the rest. It looked like the formation of geese flying overhead. The leader of the group, Thunderbird #1, initiated their turns and twists, and the other three planes followed the movements of the leader's plane strictly. Coming out of a "line-abreast loop" maneuver, Thunderbird #1 malfunctioned, and the other planes followed their leader straight into the ground. There was nothing wrong with their planes, but they followed their formation to the end. All four pilots were killed. Only one plane should have crashed, but the other pilots didn't look ahead.

> It's time to agree with what your Father God says in His Word and no longer put up with a lifestyle of just getting by.

When a family is in survival mode, the members are blind to what's approaching. They can't see the destruction somebody is leading them toward. It's easy to fall into traps and make bad decisions when you're living in a constant state of crisis. Parents are the leading planes, and the children follow. So parents, we have to ask ourselves, who are *we* following? When Gary and I switched our allegiance away from the master of fear and to the Prince of Peace, we took a turn for the better.

The first step is simple: *look up.* Wake up from survival mode so you know where you're heading. Identify the course you're on right now. Stop being too busy to reflect on where you're going. Is your family headed for a cliff? Is your marriage about to crash? Are your children going down the wrong path? Is somebody in your life leading you toward destruction?

Back away from crisis mode and take a moment to examine what is really going on in your life and where your family is aiming.

Step #2: Turn to Father God

In Judges 6, the people of Israel found themselves in an oppressed situation similar to the family in Gary's dream. They had left their world of possibilities and were hiding in strongholds and caves. Israel couldn't expand their borders or prosper while they were in hiding. They couldn't engage life. They were in survival mode, and that's a dangerous place to stay. When they tried to plant crops, their enemies destroyed their crops and killed their animals. Their enemies were so many that they looked like locusts trying to ravage their land.

The Israelites cried out to God for help, asking, "God, why did you let this happen to us? If you're supposedly with us, how did this happen?"

God sent a prophet to answer them. The prophet spoke on behalf of God, saying, "I delivered you from the hand of your oppressors; I drove them out before you and gave you their land . . . I said to you, 'Do not worship the gods of the Amorites,' *but you have not listened to me.*"

Then the Lord told Gideon, "Go in the strength you have and save Israel out of your oppressor's hand. Am I not sending you?"

"Pardon me, my Lord," Gideon replied, "but how can I save

Israel? My clan is the weakest in the land, and I am the least in my family."

God answered, "I will be with you, and you will overcome all of your oppressors."

When the Israelites turned their focus back to God, God gave them a new grace to overcome their situation. When they brought God's power back into their lives, the solution was simple: "Go save your people. I will be with you, so you will win!"

Maybe you've tried to have success in your family and finances but keep running up against enemies that are robbing you of your destiny. The confusion and pain seem oppressing and overwhelming. God is saying to you, "Go save your family! Go save your nation! I will be with you so you will win!" When you turn to God, you can defeat the enemy's attacks against your family! You can hear God's voice and receive wisdom to lead your family. When you bring God's power into your family situation, the victory is already yours!

I am always amazed that people in survival mode don't turn to God, but it's often because their situation seems too hopeless to believe there's help or that God loves them enough to rescue them. But when you get tired of living in hiding, or your family is in a real crisis, God is ready and willing to help if you just ask. You can change your family's course before you crash.

Step #3: Listen

Pay attention to what God told Israel: "I delivered you from the hand of all your oppressors; I drove them out before you and gave you their land . . . *but you have not listened to me.*"

When you cry out to God, He is going to speak to you. It's up to you to listen and simply obey His Word and allow God to reveal answers to you.

"He says, 'Be still, and know that I am God; I will be exalted among the nations, I will be exalted in the earth'" (Psalm 46:10).

If you and your family are not where you think you should be, you need to be open for God's Spirit to point out the things that may be hindering your ability to advance. You need to take God at His Word and go in the strength that you have.

Don't settle for a compromise. When God gives you His Word, you have to believe it and step out on that Word. Choose to obey and trust Him, even if it means giving up a couple of time commitments and refocusing your priorities to get your family to a healthy place. You have to move toward prayer and peace for your family.

You have enough strength with God to overcome the problems in your family. Just as it was for Gideon, God's direction will give you the encouragement and power to surpass your problems. God's grace is powerful in you, and with Him you can overcome.

Step #4: Close an Open Door

If there are destructive situations in your family, there's an open door somewhere through which Satan is entering, coming to steal, kill, and destroy (John 10:10). You shouldn't have destruction in your family. It's not normal. It's not right. It is not God's plan for you.

When I was raising my children, people told me about the "terrible twos," and how raising teenagers would be the worst. I refused to accept those cultural expectations. That's not normal! Just because the world has those outcomes does not mean you should have them in your family. My toddlers had "terrific twos," and I loved when they grew into teenagers! There are always challenges along the way, but you don't have to excuse disobedience as a "phase." If you have those consistent results with your children, there's an open door ushering that into your life. Ask God to help you identify that door so you can slam it shut.

This reminds me of a story in Joshua. After Joshua defeated the mighty fortress of Jericho, he sent only a few thousand men to take the small city called Ai. What Joshua didn't know was that there was a door opened in his army after the battle of Jericho (Joshua 7:1). His army was defeated because a man named Achan had sinned by keeping a devoted thing. The Bible says that at this the hearts of the people melted in fear and became like water.

Joshua was devastated by the loss of his men and fell on his face and cried out to God, "Why did this happen?" God answered by saying that sin had opened the door to make them "liable to destruction." Then He warned, "I will not be with you anymore unless you destroy whatever among you is devoted to destruction. You cannot stand against your enemies until you remove them."

It's the same way in your family. If there is destruction in your family, God did not do it, and it's not supposed to be there. Destruction is not right or normal. There is an open door somewhere!

God has given you the equipment and grace to have a great family life, marriage, and destiny, but you first have to know that it's yours so you

> If you and your family are not where you think you should be, you need to be open for God's Spirit to point out the things that may be hindering your ability to advance.

can pursue it. You also have to decide not to accept compromise and a mediocre lifestyle, because it's not all about you. It's about your children and your spouse, too. You are destined to win in life together.

A lot of wives nag their husbands because they realize they are going to end up where their husband ends up. When she sees her husband escaping into sports, watching baseball five nights a week or playing video games constantly, she says, "Wait a minute, we aren't going anywhere! He needs a good kick in the right direction." While it's good she has identified a problem and her concerns may be valid, when she resorts to critical words and insults, she only adds to the problem. There is a way to give wisdom without nagging, and we'll get to that later on.

Men, your families need you and your vision. You need to be the one who is calling out to God and getting the answers for your life. You are taking your family somewhere. You can't just sit there and wait. You have to say, "I want the best for my family, and I am willing to communicate with God and my wife to find it together. I want God's destiny for my family. I refuse to fail. I have the mind of Christ and wisdom for my situation. God has made me more than an overcomer!"

Husbands, you'll find that your wife and kids will follow your leadership if you do this. In fact, many times they have been waiting for that moment. Your wife will be celebrating. She wants you to have vision, spiritual integrity, and a desire to make things work. The moment she hears you say, "We're not going to live this way forever. You deserve more than this," she is going to do a happy dance! She'll start fighting to help you reach the vision.

Gideon and Joshua had to cry out to God. They both had to come to God and say, "Wait a minute, I don't like what's going on. There's destruction in our life, and that's not right. We don't want to live in defeat."

And God said, "I'm glad you're finally talking to Me about this, because I don't like it either! Here's what you need to do to close the door to destruction."

Recognize that you need Him and that you need to tear down the distractions and escapism in your life and present yourself to Him. Most of the time, God has to reestablish your foundation. Cracks in relationships are the result of a foundation issue! He is going to work in your heart, your spouse's heart, and the heart of your children. He is going to point out where your heart shifted to the wrong things. He is going to talk to you about how to love your spouse and kids and reestablish a foundation of His love in their lives, too.

God Can Do All Things

Case in point, Steve and Mindy both came into marriage with very different expectations. He was a hard worker, accustomed to having lots of extra money to spend, and she already had a son and had only enough money to pay her bills every month. On top of the everyday family stresses, as time progressed, the market crashed, they lost their incomes, credit cards were maxed out, and there was the constant threat of foreclosure and shut-off notices.

Mindy said that as they descended deeper into their problems, "We didn't just lose our way, we destroyed the path. Our house was like a ticking time bomb."

The situation escalated to the point where Steve was always angry, and they were afraid to talk to each other because even the simplest, most innocent topic ended in an argument. It was constant warfare against each other. The children were so unhappy after hearing them fight for hours about topics that kids shouldn't hear that they were silenced as well.

Mindy came to feel that Steve hated her and wished he had never met her, and vice versa. It got to the point where they didn't even want to get out of bed in the morning, even to see their three children. They wanted to give up on life. Mindy had wanted to be like June Cleaver from *Leave It to Beaver*, the perfect wife and mother, but she felt she was a total failure and fell into depression. She didn't want to do anything other than stay in bed and wait for her life to run out. The only thing that kept her from acting on her depression was her children. She worried that they would blame themselves.

Mindy says, "To say I wanted to die isn't really a good explanation, because I didn't want to die. The truth is I just didn't want to live. I was out of options. I thought the world and my family would be better off without me. Satan convinced me that I was being selfish by staying here."

At one point, Steve and Mindy actually had an argument over who was going to kill themselves. They both felt the family would be better off without them, but they didn't want to leave their children without one parent to care for them.

A parent at a middle school football banquet started bugging Steve and Mindy to come to our church. He was relentless and pestered Steve and Mindy until they finally agreed to go as long as he never asked them again. They started attending our church for the sake of their children. Weeks went by, and Steve and Mindy kept coming. More weeks past, and they started a relationship with God. As their relationship with God grew, it brought Steve and Mindy closer without them even realizing it. They began to forgive each other and treat each other better.

Five years later, and Steve and Mindy's marriage has been restored to better than ever! They have the same heart and the same mission. Their kids all love God and are serving in the Kingdom in different ways. They have seen the hopelessness their family was in and the tragic ending it was about to come to. They have witnessed the transformation in their family and seen firsthand that God can do all things. Financially, Steve and

Mindy are completely out of debt with the exception of their mortgage, which will be paid off by the end of the year.

"Act, and God Will Act"

"If any of you lacks wisdom, you should ask God, who gives generously to all without finding fault, and it will be given to you" (James 1:5).

Sometimes we get distracted, and our heart begins to callous toward hearing God's voice, and we get off the mark. Life's pressures have a way of choking out God's Word, and so we have to reestablish our relationship with God and listen for His direction. And when you cry out to God, you're going to find some changes needed in your life.

> You may be outnumbered by your problems and facing hopeless circumstances, but God has a divine plan to bring you into restoration—and you don't have to suffer any casualties.

There are always more journeys and challenges in life. We will never get to the place where we don't need to continually follow God in our lives. The moment we think we can do it alone is the time our pride will cause us to fall into a delusion that lands us back in trouble.

You may be in a place where it seems hopeless, but you and God can take on anything. Ask God to reestablish your foundation and to repurpose your family in Him. Listen for His instruction and walk it out in the strength He has given you.

Joan of Arc said it beautifully, "Act, and God will act."

When you take a step of obedience, God's grace (His power) will meet you. You won't do it alone. It is impossible to change in your strength and ability. God's power is the only way you can reclaim your identity in Christ, impact your family, and place them on the right foundation. God's power is the key to your destiny. God wants to fill your faith with His ability! You are not alone. Help is just a prayer away:

> *Father God, I come to You and ask for Your help to reestablish my family's foundation on Your Word. I humble myself before You and recognize I cannot succeed in my family or business without your direction. I ask for Your help, and I commit my life to You. I ask You to repurpose my life and help me to lead my family by Your Spirit.*

You don't have to fight the battle by yourself. Gideon's army was small in number, but with a divine plan, they won the battle without even going into war. The army of 135,000 soldiers saw Gideon's 300 men and thought they were surrounded. They began to kill *one another*, without Gideon's army suffering any casualties!

That is how God wants to work in your life. You may be outnumbered by your problems and facing hopeless circumstances, but God has a divine plan to bring you into restoration—and you don't have to suffer any casualties. Your life will make a statement!

Write a family vision statement that includes your dreams for your marriage, children, and destiny together.

....

....

....

....

....

....

What are three things that need to be changed before your family can reach that vision?

1. ....

2. ....

3. ....

James 1:5 states that if you need wisdom you should ask God and He will supply it to you. Is there anything that you need to ask God for wisdom about?

....

....

....

....

....

What can you take away from this chapter and implement in your life today? Are there any open doors you can identify that need closed?

....

....

....

....

....

The Vintage Collection
OF GOOD CHARACTER

"I have lived, sir, a long time; and the longer I
live, the more convincing proofs I see of this truth:
that God governs in the affairs of men. And if
a sparrow cannot fall to the ground without His
notice, is it probable that an empire can rise
without His aid? We have been assured, sir, in
the Sacred Writings that except the Lord build the
House, they labor in vain that build it."

BEN FRANKLIN, ADDRESSING THE CONSTITUTIONAL CONVENTION

Ben Franklin, framer of the Constitution, created a list of character traits that changed his life from a failure to great success:

SELF-CONTROL: be determined and disciplined in your efforts.

SILENCE: listen better in all discussions.

ORDER: don't agonize—organize.

PLEDGE: promise to put your best effort into today's activities.

THRIFT: watch how you spend your money and your time.

PRODUCTIVITY: work hard—work smart—have fun.

FAIRNESS: treat others the way you want to be treated.

MODERATION: avoid extremes.

CLEANLINESS: have a clean mind, body, and habits.

TRANQUILITY: take time to slow down and "smell the roses."

CHARITY: help others.

HUMILITY: keep your ego in check.

SINCERITY: be honest with yourself and others.

Gary and I with
the grandbabies.

Enjoying a beautiful
afternoon in the European
countryside.

Just What You're Looking For

BUILDING A FAMILY THAT CAN OUTLAST THE CULTURE

"The family is the cornerstone of our society. . . .
So, unless we work to strengthen the family,
to create conditions under which most parents
will stay together, all the rest—schools,
playgrounds, and public assistance and
private concern—will never be enough."
LYNDON BAINES JOHNSON

We built our dream home nearly eighteen years ago. In the building process, there were many things the builders had to take into account. They had to be sure to dig past the frost line, set the concrete at the right dimensions, and lay the foundation correctly. If they built the foundation wrong, it wouldn't matter how beautifully I furnished the inside—the foundation would be cracked and the house would fall as soon as any pressure came against it.

The foundation of the house is rarely seen, but it is the house's stability. It's the same with your family's private life—it is the foundation you are building for your children, and the truth is what happens behind closed doors. To bring your children to church or attend a Bible study looks good on the exterior, but your children will always revert and rely on their foundation—what happens at home. Your family must be built on God's Word.

Jesus said, "What you have said in the dark will be heard in the daylight, and what you have whispered in the ear in the inner rooms will be proclaimed from the roofs" (Luke 12:3). That is so apt for family life.

I observe husbands and wives tearing their own homes down by following others' foolish examples. In one case, I was in a salon with a hairstylist who had recently gone through a bitter divorce. She spoke brashly, taunting and almost demanding that her female coworkers go to a male strip club with her for the evening. They were married women, and she shamed them all into saying yes except the stylist servicing me, who leaned in to ask me, "What do I say?"

I whispered, "Tell her you're going home to the only man you want to see strip!"

She said it teasingly, but once she did, silence fell, and one by one the other women decided they better go home, too!

I was surprised how quickly the others had been bullied into doing something that would foolishly tear down their own house (family). It only took one to get them headed in the wrong direction. But it also only took one who was willing to stand up to give the others the courage to do so.

I would encourage you to not let any militant voice, whether in the media or the workplace, bully you into letting go of your family or the timeless principles that build your home when applied with love. Watch your friendships; you will become them.

We built our family in the same way we built our house. We laid a firm foundation and built upon that with sturdy materials. We have always strived to keep our family's private life congruent with what we say in our public life, because what happens in private is our foundation, and that is crucial to our children. These are the priorities we put into our family's foundation.

Priority #1: God First

Faith in Christ and His work has to be the foundation of the family. Some people have never been taught who God is and have never been introduced to His love. If that's you today, it's the first place to start. It's so simple and freeing to give your worries to a Creator who loves you. It's amazing to be able to commune with the One who started this whole family thing to begin with. God wanted a family, so He created you! Turn your life over to Him today and start to learn more about Him. It will be the best decision you ever make for your family and for yourself!

Once we turn our lives over to God, we must prioritize our relationship with Him. I had the honor of leading many of my children to the Lord by sharing with them God's love and plan for salvation. I tried to teach them scriptures each week and help them learn about God. We attended church every week so they could be taught more about God and loving His church. I realized early on that if we consistently put sporting events or ballet classes in front of God and attending church, we're demonstrating that as a priority over God to our children.

Psalm 127:1 says, "Unless the LORD builds the house, the builders labor in vain. Unless the LORD watches over the city, the guards stand watch in vain."

God should be your family's number one priority. If it is, attending your local church will naturally follow. It is important that your children see that you believe what you say you believe, when you're at home as well.

I can verbally tell you that I love my husband and we are happy together, but if you came to our house and heard us screaming at each other, you would have every reason to doubt my sincerity. If somebody tells us something that doesn't line up with the evidence, we conclude they are lying. So when you tell your children that you love God at church but don't live accordingly at home, your children begin to question God. They mistrust God, because two and two aren't adding up.

Gary and I made our fair share of mistakes as parents, but learning how to handle our mistakes was as important as learning how to handle our successes. We always tried not to argue (or have an "intense discussion" as we liked to call it) in front of the children, because that makes a child feel insecure. We tried, but we didn't always succeed. When we did argue in front of our children, we had to apologize to them for the way we behaved and we had to reaffirm our love for each other. That was important, because it made them feel safe.

Through the years, we have maintained a family day where we have fun, confirm our love for the children, and then redirect our priority to God with family prayer. Our daughter calls it "Funday Monday." It can be any day, but there must be a family day dedicated to reconnecting and refreshing with one another. You need your children's foundation to be solid, and instilling how good God is into them at a young age is the best way to do that.

We have a close family because we protected our foundation. We didn't just preach to our kids or cause our children to feel as though they had to compete with God for our attention. We invested in them first, and then as a family, we would pray. We discussed the things we believed for, and the children each took turns praying for those things, and we would write the prayer requests down in what we called our James 4 Notebook.

Then they got to watch them come to pass! It was great because it gave them evidence of God's faithfulness.

Priority #2: Respect for Your Spouse

Love and respect for your spouse is the priority next to God that your children need to see. A lot of parents miss this, because they place their children over their marriage. When you place your children over the health of your marriage, you actually damage both in the long run!

I learned long ago that you never take the complaints and disagreements you have with your spouse to your children. That is a big *no-no*! Your children need to respect and obey your spouse, but when you dump all the negative complaints from your marriage onto

> You need your children's foundation to be solid, and instilling how good God is into them at a young age is the best way to do that.

your child, you can't expect them to respect your spouse—or you. Your marriage is a large portion of your family dynamic, and even if your spouse is not living right, you can set the right example for your children. I delve deeper into this topic in the chapter about *Doing Life Tandem*, but I want to briefly touch on it here.

Your marriage lays a foundation for your children. Whether you respect your spouse or you talk negatively about them lays a foundation for your children. If you're undermining your spouse's authority or disrespecting them in front of your kids, you can expect the same behavior from your children toward your spouse, *yourself,* and other people in authority. You're giving them the OK on this kind of behavior, and the fruit of that will show in their life.

Ask yourself: *What kind of foundation do I want to set through my marriage?*

Priority #3: Honor Family

When Gary and I went into ministry, I had a wrong perception about where the family fit. I saw so many ministry families in shambles, and I thought that ministry meant sacrificing time with my children. I prayed, "God, I want to serve You through ministry, but I can't give up my children."

I'll never forget what God told me. "I never asked you to."

That was an amazing revelation to me! God doesn't want to steal me away from my children. God wants me to be with my family as much as I do. God created my family and wants to protect it. *Wow!*

When you realize how sacred your family is to God, you understand how important it is that you fight for your family. God *wants* you to fight for your family—it's biblical!

God created your family to bless you, not to curse you. God loves families, and He wants to operate through them to change nations, as He did with Abraham's family, Noah's family, and Mary and Joseph's family! Family is a powerful thing. That's why Satan hates families, and that's why you have to protect your family time.

It's important that at least once a week you put everything on pause and focus on your family. Don't let your job, extracurricular activities, or ministry come between you and your family. God wants your family whole more than He wants you to volunteer. God is your first priority, then marriage, then family, and then any ministry activities, jobs, or sports events.

Gary and I decided that if our ministry is ever hurting our family, we will quit because family is our first priority. Our children and their perspective of God are more important than other ministry opportunities. And there have been a couple of times when we had to reevaluate how much time we were putting into ministry versus how much time we were spending with our children. We had to recheck our priorities to protect our family.

If you're not making your family a priority, I can tell you, Satan is, and he is seeking whom he may devour. He wants to get you too busy, too stressed, and too rundown to make your family a priority. If you're too busy to keep these three priorities in your life, you're too busy! You need to carve out time for more of what really matters in your life!

The Four Building Blocks to Every Family

The foundation and structure you set for your children is like a table. It should be built on four legs to create a good foundation, and those four pillars hold up the family. Those four pillars are *discipline*, *love*, *faith*, and *example*. When you have a balance of all four pillars in your family, your family can stand strong even when obstacles and pressure come against you.

> If you're not making your family a priority, I can tell you, Satan is, and he is seeking whom he may devour.

Continuing with this metaphor (I'm a woman, so of course I can speak fluent furniture metaphors), the centerpiece of your table should be God. That is what your table should be built around. That happens because your family obeys God. Your foundation should be focused on God. Everything you do and every decision you make should be centered on God. You have to decorate your table in accordance with your centerpiece—otherwise you get tempted to throw out that centerpiece and get a new one that matches the rest of your decor.

That is what people do with God. They set Him as their centerpiece, but then they like something that doesn't match up with His Word, and they start adding things to their table that don't line up. Eventually, they have to repent and clean the table, or else they throw out the centerpiece altogether.

Discipline

The first pillar that your family should be built on is *discipline*. It is so important that I will expand on it later. For now, let me just assure you how important discipline is. In fact, the Bible says that you hate your children if you don't discipline them (Proverbs 13:24). The Bible is black and white on this subject. Nothing says it stronger than Proverbs 19:18: "Discipline your children, for in that there is hope; do not be a willing party to their death."

Wow! Do you want to be a willing party to the death of your children? When you look at discipline in this light, and you keep the vision before you, it makes it easier to make the hard choices while parenting. The next time you don't feel like disciplining your child, remember that you don't want to be a willing party to their death.

I know those scriptures don't correlate with many people's ideals of tolerance, but I choose the Word of God over the opinions of man. Discipline is driven by love, not violence. Discipline is there to help your children—it's not abuse and should never be carried to that kind of level. The law kills and destroys, but the spirit of life in Christ Jesus brings liberty. When there is an understanding of restraint, personal restraint, there's liberty.

One time I was riding in the car with friends, and their little girl was throwing a screaming tantrum in the backseat. The girl's siblings tossed her toys to try to entertain her, but when she didn't quiet down, the siblings were blamed by the parents. It got to the point where I couldn't take it anymore. I asked my friend to pull the car over, and I looked at the father and said, "If you let her scream like that, she is going to learn to be selfish and expect other people to pamper her the rest of her life. You better discipline her!"

Many families pamper and spoil one child, giving them everything they want without boundaries. Then, when the next child comes along, the older one is dethroned. Suddenly the older child has to care and cater to the younger one's every need and fix their problems. The parents get strict with the older child and let the younger one get away with treason, creating a sibling rivalry.

It's easier to try to get a child to stop crying by giving them something or entertaining them than to deal with the root issue, but it's not effective. Children are smarter than you think, and the younger child will learn to expect others to cater to their wants.

One of our children discovered that Gary and I were less likely to discipline them when we were at the mall or in public. I was shopping alone when one of my children started throwing a tantrum in the store—dragging on the ground, whining, and the whole works. So here I was, in the middle of shopping, and I didn't know what to do. People were staring at me. Moms gave me sympathetic smiles, some people made comments just loud enough for me to overhear about the noise my child was making, and others raised their eyebrows and looked on in shock. I was too embarrassed to respond. While I didn't want to give up my shopping trip to deal with the issue, I decided that mentoring my child was more important than my shopping list. I left the store, screaming child in tow. I wouldn't let my children manipulate me by acting out in public.

I often see moms in stores who are not doing anything about a child who's throwing a tantrum. The next time the child wants something, they know all they have to do is take the situation to a public level. On the other hand, you always need to use wisdom. If you have your child out shopping an hour after their bedtime, and they are fussy, you need to take that child home for bed.

The revelation of discipline in your family life, and how to do it the right way, can completely transform your family. The important thing is that it needs to be done the *right* way, and that's where so many people get offtrack. I will dive into the topic in greater detail at a later point, but for now just understand that discipline done in the right way is a part of God's plan, and it is necessary to the health of your family.

Love

The second pillar of the table is *love*. I purposefully put love next to discipline, because love balances discipline out. They go hand-in-hand. You should never discipline without love, and discipline should never derive out of anything other than love.

On occasion one of our children has approached Gary and me and said, "My friend is allowed to do such-and-such, so I should be allowed to." My response is, "I love you too much to say yes to that." We didn't apologize to our child for choosing what is right and protecting them from the corruption of the world. Love says yes to the right things, and no to the wrong things. When you love your children, you choose good and healthy things for them.

What can your children say to that? How can your children argue against being loved?

We model how much we love our kids by the boundaries we set for them. Children want parents who love them enough to confront them for acting out. They might not thank you for it in the moment, but they will respect you in the long run. Don't let them play the "everyone else is doing it" card on you. That is manipulation, and you love them too much to allow them to manipulate their way around accountability.

I always tried to make things in our home fun for our kids. If you're harsh or always angry with your kids, you're going to cause them to rebel against God. Nobody wants to be in that kind of environment.

Without love, discipline turns to abuse. Your children will resent you for discipline that is not acting out of love, and that's why the two go hand-in-hand. When Gary or I spanked our children, we always started out by explaining why we had to spank them. We explained what they did, and how much we loved them. After we spanked them, we gave them a hug and reaffirmed our love. That is crucial. If you don't reaffirm your love after discipline, your children feel separated from you and could form resentment.

> We model how much we love our kids by the boundaries we set for them.

Many parents fall on the legalistic side, only giving their children rules and regulations and never doing anything to affirm their love. Your children will begrudge you if the only time you show up is to say no to them. If children then realize the only time you give them attention is when they misbehave, they will do bad things to at least get some sort of attention. Love and discipline must be balanced. You can do and should do fun things with your children, and it doesn't have anything to do with money. On the flipside, buying them expensive things doesn't equal quality time and attention from you. They need your time, not an open line of credit. Borrow camping equipment and get out there. Do the best you can with what you have and have fun!

A lot of parents are afraid to tell their children the truth. They are afraid that if they are honest, their child will turn from

God, so they embrace their sin instead. Love does not ignore the truth; love is your mission to spread it. If you love someone, you will tell them the truth. You need to be honest and say, "According to my personal conviction and God's Word, this is wrong. I'm not going to badger you about it or keep bringing it up, but it's important that you know where I stand. I love you, and I care about you deeply, but this is sin."

Love is the glue that holds together a family. We all make mistakes—parents and children alike say or do the wrong things—but love ties us together. First Peter 4:8 says, "Above all, love each other deeply, because love covers over a multitude of sins."

Faith and Example

The third pillar of the family is *faith*, because the family unit loses its impact when it's apart from God. Your children need to grow up experiencing God in their life.

And the fourth pillar, which may be the most underestimated, is *example*. Example whittles down to the very core of your family's foundation: what your children *experience* speaks louder than your words. Example covers anywhere from the example you set for your children at home, or from your children experiencing a relationship with God and His faithfulness for themselves.

I combine the third and fourth pillars because whenever you combine faith and example, you get one of the most powerful of principles: *faith by example.* It's one thing to tell your children about God, but when they experience God in their life and witness faith in action, it's the most life-changing experience available. Your example of faith in the life of your children can change the whole picture.

Gary's father, Tom, was a cynical man who never hesitated to voice his disapproval of God or the church. It got to the point where we avoided talking about the ministry around him at all costs. Gary said he didn't know if he had the faith for his father to get saved—his father was so opposed to the gospel and so hard-hearted that Gary couldn't see beyond that. What could Gary say that would make a difference? There were no words to reach him. We'd used them all.

Years went by, and nothing changed. Gary and I continued in ministry and started broadcasting on television. Gary still couldn't imagine his father saved. He kept praying that God would send someone else to minister to his father, but there was no hint of change. In a huge turn of events, when Gary's father was eighty years old, he came to church on a Sunday morning, gave his life to the Lord, and made the most dramatic transformation we have ever seen. He went and apologized to everyone he had ever wronged in his life and was a different man from that day forward. For the next three years of his life he attended church almost every weekend and shared the good news of God, and he went home to be with his Lord at the age of eighty-three.

So why did he come to church on that Sunday? What made a man who critically attacked faith much of his life suddenly decide to give his life to the Lord? We didn't know it, but Tom had been watching our television broadcast for months! He started watching his son tell stories of healing, restoration, and financial turnarounds. He had witnessed our lives as we went from poverty and mounds of debt to provision. He witnessed our daughter healed of a tumor overnight, losing thirteen pounds and nine inches in her waist instantly. When someone asked him why he finally decided to give his heart to Christ, he simply replied, "I saw too much that I couldn't explain."

Faith by *example*. It's a powerful combination.

When words can't reach someone, it is the evidence of God's goodness that catches people's attention. You can preach to your children around the clock, but the example you are portraying speaks louder than your words. Your greatest testimony in life is often not the story you tell with words, but the one you tell through what you do. You can minister to others simply by living your life according to God's Word. There's an old quote that says, "Actions prove who someone is. Words prove who they want to be."

Joseph in the Bible put this principle into action. Growing up, he was the favorite son of his father in a large family, and his brothers despised him for it. One day they captured him and sold him into slavery. Taken to Egypt, Joseph worked as a slave in Potiphar's house and so excelled that he was put in charge of the household. But when Joseph denied the sexual advances of Potiphar's wife, she falsely accused him and had him thrown into prison with a life sentence. Without any hope of getting out of the prison, Joseph continued to portray faith by example and was put in charge of managing the prison.

> It's one thing to tell your children about God, but when they experience God in their life and witness faith in action, it's the most life-changing experience available.

People can't deny the evidence of faith and the fruit of faithfulness. Joseph's day came when he interpreted Pharaoh's dream and was elevated to Pharaoh's right hand man who oversaw all of Egypt. Joseph's *life* ministered to all around him, including his brothers when they came to Egypt for food. They found out that he was now the second highest ranked man in Egypt, and Joseph was able to minister to the very people who tried to destroy him—all because his life was an example of his faith. You see, people can't argue against the evidence of faith. That is why you need to have that principle working on your behalf in your family.

The foundation you build your family on defines the kind of structure that can rise out of that foundation. The priorities you establish with your children in action speak louder than the priorities you talk about. You can declare the importance of attending church, but do you consistently attend church? Your actions set the bar.

These powerful principles will transform your life. Ask God for wisdom as we move forward in identifying areas to grow in and impart into your family.

I love family dinners!

Yesterday's Farmhouse

Today's Dream Home

Are your priorities in order? Why or why not?

....
....
....
....
....

Is there one priority or pillar you need to work on? How can you do that?

....
....
....
....
....
....

Are you laying the right foundation in your family's private life?

....
....
....
....
....

What can you take away from this chapter and apply to your everyday life?

....
....
....
....
....

Amy's
MONOGRAPH
MY FIRSTBORN

"Mom! There's a snake on the back porch!" yelled my brother Tom, running wildly into the living room. My mom's face said it all. She went out to the back porch to find my brother Tim dissecting said snake, and Tim went on to describe each part to her. Being a homeschooling family, Mom at least had the satisfaction of knowing that Tim had paid attention in biology.

It's funny to look back at that incident and think of how I would react, now that I am a mom. My mom didn't get upset, uptight, or angry that her sons had killed and dissected a snake. She was a little disgusted at the sight, but she encouraged and praised them for their curiosity and bravery.

I find myself in situations with my two toddlers and think, *How would my mom react to this?* She was and is good at encouraging the giftings in others and pushing them toward their God-given destiny.

The snake story was a telling example of my brothers' very different giftings and personalities. Tom was excited about capturing and killing the evil snake. Today he is a spiritual warrior, musician, and producer with an evangelistic bend. He has an intensity against our enemy Satan that scares hell, I'm sure! Tim has a pastoral gifting and is a visionary leader who likes to find out how things work and make them better. He also likes to break down the Word of God for others to understand easily, and he isn't afraid to get a little messy if needed. My mom recognized those giftings in her sons and took every opportunity, however unexpected, to reinforce and encourage those areas of their lives.

For me, I am the firstborn and the natural "second mom" to the troupe. I was the peacemaker and a little bossy to my siblings, but my overall goal growing up was to make sure everyone was happy. I was also extremely shy, and my mom knew that my calling would require me being in front of people, so she gave me a little extra encouragement to overcome some of my shyness. From the age of six I went around the house constantly singing and writing songs, so a few years later she took me to a tryout for a kids' choir. Once I was accepted into the choir, she tirelessly drove me to rehearsals and performances, shopped for deals when specific clothing was needed, cheered me on when I succeeded, and got in my face with scriptures when I wanted to quit. I'm so thankful for that tenacity today, because I lead worship and oversee a team of musicians. I'm the team "mom" for sure, but when it comes time to get in God's presence, I'm not afraid or shy to do so boldly.

As parents, we have been entrusted with such a precious prize: the lives of eternal souls. My little girl, Journey, is very much like me, with some of her daddy's leadership qualities mixed in there. My little son, Dawson, is so strong and yet sweet and sensitive, full of curiosity and a bend toward the mechanical workings of things. I already see the giftings in them starting to be revealed, day-by-day. How amazing that the seeds of greatness are already inside their little spirits, just waiting to be watered and cultivated. I am amazed that God trusts me with these jewels, and even on the tough days when there's food flung all over the kitchen and the laundry is piled high, I am thankful. I have such an important voice in their lives and in their destinies. In fact, whomever they influence and reach in their lifetime will be credited to my heavenly account, too, if I do my job well.

In our fast-paced world full of a plethora of distractions, how easy is it to overlook a seed? Very. But such power lies within that seed! Think about it. Your child has the power to change lives, build the Kingdom of God, restore hope, tear down strongholds, and bring heaven to earth! That's the seed of greatness in our children. Yet, in my daily tasks, challenges, activities, responsibilities, and entertainments, I can leave that seed unwatered and untended. I can neglect those seeds of greatness through my careless words, my angry gestures, my own selfishness or self-importance, and my stress.

This doesn't mean we have to be at our children's beck and call with unlimited resources, giving them everything they want 24 hours a day. My parents certainly didn't do that. But it does mean that there needs to be an unlimited supply of love and encouragement flowing from our lips and our actions, and we need to point our children to an unlimited God. My parents did that well.

It means we have to rely heavily on the Spirit of God inside of us so that we can properly water the seeds in their spirits. It means that we need to set aside quality time with our kids without the television on, our cell phone in our hands, or our to-do list in our minds. It means we need to intentionally ask God to show us how to cultivate and grow those seeds in each of our children. We need to ask God how to be wise gardeners.

Our children are called to inherit and occupy a certain spiritual territory during their lifetime, and that's why God gave them a distinct personality, gift, and ability. No one else can fit that special spot in God's heart as well as propel His plan for this earth. They are uniquely crafted to meet a special need. We as parents are the catapults that fling them toward their future in Christ! I know, it sounds daunting and scary, but we aren't alone.

> As parents, we have been entrusted with such a precious prize: the lives of eternal souls.

Psalm 25:12 NLT is a command and a promise. It says, "Who are those who fear the LORD? He will show them the path they should choose. They will live in prosperity, and their children will inherit the land."

God will show us the path to take. The requirement? That we fear Him. What does it mean to "fear the LORD," and how do we do that as parents? I believe it means that we care about God's opinion more than anyone else's. It means we reverence and worship God and respect His parenting methods over the world's. People have some strange notions when it comes to parenting, and we need to place a higher value on God's way of doing things, no matter the persecution that may come from people who don't understand it. Jesus must be our example as the perfect Shepherd, and God's Word must be our parenting manual. It's easy enough to find parenting advice online, but how about we take our parenting advice straight from the perfect Father?

I want prosperity for my children! I want them to succeed and inherit the earth! Those are God's desires for us! So my job is to constantly turn to my Father God and follow His example in parenting. He knows what our children need even when we overlook it. He knows what we need even before we do. He will show us how. He will encourage us when we blow it. He will give us the master gardening tips, because, after all, He is the Master Gardener.

Big sisters love you till it hurts.

A naive couple that
loves God embarks
on their journey
May 10, 1982.

The day I married
my best friend!
August 7, 1982.

The Family Mission

THE FAMILY'S ROLE IN GOD'S REVIVAL PLAN

"This is the crisis we're in: God-light streamed into the world, but men and women everywhere ran for the darkness. They went for the darkness because they were not really interested in pleasing God."

JOHN 3:19 MSG

Why write a book about family life? Years ago, shortly after I became a committed believer in Christ, I heard a message preached that rocked my world—the kind that catches you completely off guard and leaves you undone by the presence of God, knowing you will never be the same. I was so struck by the words in Malachi 2:15, "Has not the one God made you? You belong to him in body and spirit. And what does the one God seek? Godly offspring. So be on your guard, and do not be unfaithful to the wife of your youth."

My years of feminist training—to reject marriage and family

as a less than noble pursuit, compared to the ventures of making money or becoming famous—all melted away in a powerful encounter with God. The One God was seeking godly children? None of my peers was seeking children! That encounter resulted in a complete change of pursuits for me. I was suddenly aware that this idea of family, being in God's family and creating a godly family, was near and dear to God's heart. Through a transformation it became near to my heart, too. But I didn't know how to accomplish it. I just knew it was worth pursuing!

Throughout the last fifty years or more our country lost the importance and foundation for family. Almost every problem we see today is a result of family problems and issues. Yet the more problems we have, the less focus or interest in family. People have become more self-absorbed, and as a result, we've been spiraling downward as a nation, as individuals and families. It's time to change that!

Today, I am the mother of five accomplished adult children, and multiplying grandchildren, not to mention many spiritual daughters and sons as well. My goal many years ago is the same today, that my children, and now grandchildren, would prophesy, which means *to speak and demonstrate the power of God.* I believe in each of their own ways, they are doing just that, and I am thrilled to see them on their own faith journeys as they build a life of vintage values, too.

Love is the greatest thing one can experience, and love begins in a family. We were not made to have a relationship with technology and self-absorption. God made us for family—His family and the one we would create with Him.

I remember a time when we were in Taco Bell eating lunch as a family. We prayed over our food, ate, and talked. Afterward, a couple approached Gary and me. The lady had tears welling in her eyes.

"I've never seen a family like yours," she said. "The whole meal my husband and I couldn't do anything but watch your family. I've never seen kids get along with their parents like yours, or talk and get along with one another so well. What's your secret?"

We had an opportunity to share God's love with that woman. We didn't have to go to her table and preach to her. Our family opened a door for us to witness simply by being ourselves. People want good families!

How sad that a functional family is an anomaly, a rarity! But that's why your family needs to shine in this time. The light shines brightest in the greatest darkness. We aren't a perfect family, so don't expect yours to be perfect either, but we tried every day to cultivate an atmosphere of love and peace.

Whether people realize it or not, they yearn for the vintage family model! Shows such as *Duck Dynasty* and others with lots of kids and family life are so popular because they give a glimpse into families that relate, that are real, working through problems, not running from them. Amidst so much dysfunction, people are craving healthy relationships.

Origins and Issues

So how did this family thing get started? How did families become so messed up in the first place? That is exactly where we need to start—with the first family, Adam and Eve. Their lives were perfect! God created everything they would need to live without fear, without sickness, without hunger, and they had each other in perfect harmony. Can you imagine being married to the perfect man or woman? I mean, they didn't have to worry about body fat, making rent, or even what they were going to wear that day. But along came Satan, a fallen angel who despised the place of authority that God had given them. You see, Satan was already on the earth when God created Adam and Eve, and he considered the earth his. God gave Adam and Eve authority to rule over the entire earth on behalf of His Kingdom (Hebrews 2:7–8). Satan didn't have the deed to the earth, Adam did.

God crowned Adam with authority (as referenced in Hebrews 2), which gave him the strength to rule. God was essentially saying, "I will back up your every word." The entire Kingdom of God, His power, and every angel backed up what Adam said on the earth, because Adam was part of God's family. He was a king's kid.

Satan despised this creation that ruled over him and knew the only way to gain control over Adam and the earth realm was for Adam to take the crown off, to give up his authority. Satan had no power to take the crown from Adam, so he had to find a way to entice Adam to actually relinquish the crown. To do that he managed to deceive Adam and Eve into believing that they could not trust God and that they should rebel against His authority and government. His temptation revolved around one tree in the garden, the only thing that Adam was told he could not have, the tree of the knowledge of good and evil. Adam and Eve were not to eat from that tree. Adam did eat of it and lost his position of authority and his ability to rule or reign over Satan in life (Genesis 3).

What happened next is the part that I want you to focus on, because it gives us a clear view of the current state that exists between men and women today. When God confronted Adam after his rebellion, instead of taking personal responsibility, Adam blamed God and his wife. When God confronted Eve about her sin, she blamed the serpent (Satan) for deceiving her. And the blame game continues to this day. Our culture is full of entitlement and victim mentalities. We all need to remember that as long as we blame others for our issues and don't take personal responsibility, we remove ourselves from God's provision and His correction, forgiveness, and restoration. By turning our backs on God as Adam and Eve did, we are doomed to repeat our sin and mistakes and duplicate them in our children.

Adam and Eve's rejection of God's authority left them and the entire earth realm under the dominion of Satan and outside of God's ability to provide for them. Life changed, not because God wanted it to, but because Adam and Eve had rejected God's provision and tied His hands legally, leaving them on their own with the result of their rebellion.

"Cursed is the ground *because of you*; *through painful toil* you will eat food from it all the days of your life. It will produce thorns and thistles for you, and you will eat the plants of the field. *By the sweat of your brow* you will eat your food until you return to the ground, since from it you were taken; for dust you are and to dust you will return" (Genesis 3:17–19).

Having lost the provision of God in the garden, where everything was already provided, Adam was now forced to find a way to survive on his own. The earth realm now would require painful toil and labor for it to produce. The harsh reality of this weight and the fear it produced caused Adam to lose sight of anything else, and survival would now become his daily routine and priority.

Things also changed for Eve as she was told how these changes would affect her in the future. "I will make your pains in childbearing very severe; with painful labor you will give birth to children. Your *desire will be for your husband*, and *he will rule over you*" (Genesis 3:16).

These two scriptures clearly define the problem between men and women. God had designed the family system to be a blessing, but now it was corrupted by sin. We find the first family in dysfunction—two broken individuals, blaming each other and God for what had just happened. The man is toiling and laboring to survive, while the woman is trying to get his attention. But she finds him preoccupied, and her continued plea for his time is largely unanswered. Sadly, she finds he is ruling her, but not loving her.

Adam and Eve had two sons, Cain and Abel (Genesis 4), who had a sibling rivalry issue, and not a small one, either. In fact, despite God's direct warning to stop his sin of jealousy, Cain murdered Abel! The very first family was full of dysfunction!

> As long as we blame others for our issues and don't take personal responsibility, we remove ourselves from God's provision and His correction, forgiveness, and restoration.

That was the second family breakdown and clear evidence of the earth curse that Adam's sin had initiated. That curse has been working against families ever since. However, God did not stand by and let His children be destroyed by Satan. He sent His own Son Jesus to reclaim the family from the curse of sin, to refashion us in His glory and repurpose His plan for families. Jesus' death paid the legal debt owed by Adam's sin and now allows us to tap into God's grace, His power and wisdom, so we can overcome the curse that Adam brought upon the earth. We can now have peace in our families and our families can be blessed *if* we say yes to Him and His plan!

"Christ has rescued us from the curse pronounced by the law. When he was hung on the cross, he took upon himself the curse for our wrongdoing. For it is written in the Scriptures, 'Cursed is everyone who is hung on a tree'" (Galatians 3:13 NLT).

God wants to help your family overcome the curse of sin. If you're willing to listen, He will impart to you the knowledge to overcome the same rut of sin and the same mistakes and dysfunction the family has cycled through since Adam's time. He will show you what He has intended the family system to look like—and He will help you live it!

The family is the building block of God's kingdom and should naturally display His righteousness. In simple terms, the family, living God's way, looks appealing, whole, and healthy to those still trapped under the curse. It is a beacon of light in a dark world. Our own families are depending on us to get it right, learning what family life is all about. We also have generations coming after us that need to know the truth. The good news is all of this is now possible through what Jesus did on the cross. We can have great families!

God's Plan for Families

God wants to talk about family, but we need to understand exactly what God's plan for family looks like and why it's so important to Him.

Have you ever noticed entire Bible passages dedicated to genealogy, such as Matthew 1:2–3, "Abraham was the father of Isaac, Isaac the father of Jacob . . ."? Why are genealogies in the Bible? Who cares what family someone came from? Is there more to family than most people recognize? Yes, there is! The Bible says that "all Scripture is God-breathed" (2 Timothy 3:16). Genealogies are in the Bible for a reason, and that reason is the key to unlocking God's purpose for your family.

For Jesus to come to earth, God would have to place His seed in the womb of a girl named Mary. But as things stood under spiritual law, that would be illegal for God to interfere, as He had given the earth realm to Adam to rule. But if He could find a man who would be willing to offer up his only son on behalf of God, that would make it legal for God to reciprocate. That man was Abraham, and his role in this plan was crucial.

Abraham and his wife were well past childbearing years and unable to have children, but God gave them a son named Isaac. God did an unusual thing, though, when He asked Abraham to take his only son and offer him as a sacrifice on the mountain. God had a better plan in mind, but He couldn't tell Abraham yet. As we look at the story of Abraham taking his son Isaac up the mountain (Genesis 22), we find some common denominators in the story when compared to the crucifixion of Jesus. Isaac's walk up the mountain and Jesus' walk to the cross both take place on the exact same mountain. Jesus was also sacrificed on the same spot that Abraham was about to slay Isaac. Jesus carried His own wooden cross to the place of His sacrifice, and Isaac carried his own wooden altar to the place of his purposed sacrifice. The death of Isaac was not finally required, but Abraham's willingness was.

When Abraham lifted his hand to slay Isaac, spiritual law was satisfied. It would now be legal for Jesus to be placed in Mary's womb, be born in the world, and be the sacrifice that was needed to set men and women free.

When God found Abraham, a man who had believed Him, God set in place a legal binding agreement between Abraham, his heirs, and Himself. This agreement was called a covenant, and it laid out promises that God would bring to pass through Abraham and his heirs as well as the requirements for those promises.

Notice that this legal agreement was set in place by one man, Abraham, but was carried by his heirs or families until the day that Jesus was born. Since the promise was made to the heirs of Abraham, Jesus *had* to come from the heirs of Abraham.

The genealogy in the first chapter of Matthew may seem boring, but in reality that chapter wasn't written for us. It was written for Satan to acknowledge that Jesus' coming to the earth was legal. It traces with minute detail that in fact Jesus was the legal descendant of Abraham, which then made His birth and sacrifice legal in the earth realm.

So how important was family in this story? It was everything. It's why Abraham was chosen in the first place. "For I have chosen him, so that he will direct his children and his household after him to keep the way of the LORD by doing what is right and just, so that the LORD will bring about for Abraham what he has promised him" (Genesis 18:19). The promise was totally dependent on Abraham and his family and on the families that followed. That was God's plan for family—they were the carrier of salvation! And when you realize God's plan, you can see that the Bible is largely a book about Jesus' family.

> When children are trained up in God's system, they don't want to go anywhere else.

Most Christians live as though that was God's *entire* plan, though. They think that God just wanted to send Jesus to die on the cross, and now we are living in the finished work. If there still isn't a plan now, we wouldn't have any purpose to stay on the earth and would have been taken up to heaven as soon as we got saved. We weren't, though, because God's plan is just as active today as it was two thousand years ago! That wasn't the finale—that was only the setup!

God restored us back to ground zero legally, as it was in the Garden of Eden, and now we are supposed to go from there. That's not the destination; that's the launching point of a new plan.

John 3:16 says, "For God so loved the world that he gave his one and only Son, that whosoever shall believe in him shall not perish but have eternal life."

Jesus was sent to the world to save mankind. My question to you is: Who is God sending now? If God so loved the world then, does He love it any less now?

God is sending us to spread His love with a hurting world that has rejected Him. That's a big responsibility. It happens through you and me, and generation by generation touching the world. Just as God wanted to protect families so Jesus could save us from our sins, so we must protect families today. Families create a foundation for the salvation of the next generation.

Abraham was chosen based on his ability to raise a godly family that later Jesus Christ would come through as a descendant. So who has God entrusted His plan with? *Families*—just like yours and mine. The family is where children learn about values, what life is, and how it functions. It's where people discern what is right and wrong and learn how to live in daily relationships.

The Family Revival

When children are trained up in God's system, they don't want to go anywhere else. It's a good system! God is good! The problem is, who knows how to train a child up? My son-in-law jokes, "They didn't come with a manual, did they?" God did give you a manual for parenting, and that's His Word.

Your children are supposed to be mentored, and that means "consistent pressure." It's kind of like weeding your garden. You watch over it and pull out the weeds. You grow and water it, anticipating the fruit it will have. That is what training is about. It's not as much what you say as what you do.

We have to be aware that God has given us the responsibility to raise our families because His plan depends on it. The family is so important to God that He says if you can't get that right, you can't stand up to your potential. In fact, the apostle Paul says, "The overseer must be above reproach . . . He must manage his own household well, with all dignity keeping his children submissive, for if someone does not know how to manage his own household, how will he care for God's church?" (1 Timothy 3:2–5 ESV).

In other words, Paul says a person is disqualified if they can't take care of their family. If they can't manage the responsibility of their family, they can't handle anything beyond that. And if somebody who can't take care of their own family does take on more, he is going to spread the dysfunction in his home to others.

Being a perfect parent is not the point—the point is that God wants us to know how He designed families to operate. And for many of us, our prosperity, our direction, and the assignment on our lives are held in check until God can trust us with our family and His destiny plan. God is training parents while they are training their children.

The world is not going to teach you how to train up your family or how to be a good husband or a wife. The world doesn't have a clue! We live in a world of selfishness. People have no understanding of sacrifice or what it means to do things righteously, unless they learn it from God and your example.

Having the hearts right in a family is so important. Luke 1:17 says, speaking of John the Baptist who came before Jesus, "And he will go on before the Lord, in the spirit and power of Elijah, to turn the hearts of the parents to their children and the disobedient to the wisdom of the righteous—to make ready a people prepared for the Lord."

Part of John the Baptist's mission was to have a family revival! God was about to launch Jesus into the earth, and God wanted to have the families intact so they were prepared to take the message of the gospel from generation to generation.

Eighty-three percent of people who accept Jesus do so before they turn fourteen years old. Only four percent accept Jesus after their thirtieth birthday.[9] Can you see the significance of the mentoring process at home toward the Kingdom of God if only four percent come to the Lord after their thirtieth birthday?

There is nothing more precious than family to God, and there's nothing more precious than family to you. There's nothing that hurts as much as having family problems and nothing as great as having family success. Family is important.

So does God still give out His assignments to those He can trust with the next generation? I believe He does. If you raise your children correctly, there is a great reward with that. There's a peace with that. I believe that your family is worth fighting for. God is depending on you to do just that!

Do you think your family has been acting on God's plan for family?

....

....

....

....

....

What role would you like to see your family step into or continue in?

....

....

....

....

....

....

Understanding the importance of family in God's plan, does this change how you will parent? What do you want to change?

....

....

....

....

....

What are some specific outreach-minded actions you would like to see in your family?

....

....

....

....

....

....

PART 2

The Vintage Life

PRINCIPLES THAT WILL CHANGE YOUR FAMILY LIFE

A misty day on our European adventure with my (Drenda's) parents for their 50th anniversary!

Gary and I in front of the Now Center that faith built!

Teamwork on our tandem bike—100 miles around the breathtaking Lake Tahoe in California and Nevada.

Doing Life Tandem

COUPLES WORKING TOGETHER

"Marriage: Love is the reason. Lifelong friendship is the gift. Kindness is the cause. 'Til death do us part is the length."

DAWN WEAVER

We've all watched a romantic movie, sighed, and thought, *If only I had a romantic life.* Hollywood gives us unrealistic expectations of romance, but Hollywood isn't real life! Romance stories cannot portray the lifetime journey, commitment, and sacrifices of a lasting lifetime marriage relationship. At the movies, in less than two hours, it appears that everything works into a perfectly crafted romantic relationship. The reality is, it takes a lifetime of growing, changing, and becoming one in marriage. Don't let the Hollywood portrayal make you feel something is missing in your marriage. What is missing in the movie version is the time, commitment, and work that make a relationship thrive. It takes more than a chick flick can reflect to build a great marriage, and the good news is your love can last much longer than a Hollywood romance!

Marriage is the bedrock of the family, so I would be amiss not to touch on vintage love. Today, more and more children are growing up with one parent, divorced parents, stepparents, and all kinds of different family dynamics. My heart breaks for the millions of men and women who have experienced the death of a marriage. Yes, God can still work through those family situations to bring amazing outcomes, despite any hurt or trauma from the past. But I also believe in doing whatever I can to prevent those types of situations from increasing. The marriage is an important aspect in the family, and I want to show you how that union can thrive using the vintage family model.

Love and Respect

It may sound silly, but when I think of marriage, the old Dudley Do-Right cartoons pop in my head. Dudley Do-Right is portrayed as a good-doing airhead who is always tricked by his arch nemesis, Snidely Whiplash. In each episode Dudley Do-Right's girlfriend, Nell, is captured by Snidely Whiplash and tied to the train tracks. She turns on her damsel-in-distress-imitation, yelling, "Oh, save me! Save me!" Of course, Dudley comes riding in on his horse to the rescue and eventually succeeds in saving Nell. And after she's saved, who does Nell thank? Dudley Do-Right's horse!

This is a funny perspective on the way couples interact. Husbands are trying to be the hero of the family by working to provide for the family's needs. And still, many wives don't recognize their husband as a hero, and they misplace their affection. Instead of praising the husband who is providing, many wives praise the horse. They praise their husband's job, or his boss, or even his money, but they fail to recognize that their husband is the one who is working to care for his family. He's the hero.

But when it comes to the downfall of marriages, there's a lot of blame to be handed out to all parties. For instance, we have a man problem in America. From generations before us that dropped the ball, we now have a large group of next generation men still living in their parents' basements, afraid of responsibility. Perhaps that partially stems from the attitude depicted in the Dudley Do-Right cartoons, where Dudley is made out to be stupid and ignorant. A great deal of the problems with men giving up on their destinies starts with the lack of respect they are given in the culture, and yes, from women.

During the feminist movement, when men lost their place as the leaders in the workplace, women adopted the mindset, "Anything you can do, I can do better." Women started tearing down men and trying to elevate themselves instead. Along with that mentality, the culture created the persona that men were naive and ignorant. The media still has an anti-male movement, which is strategic and dangerous to the family system. Satan does not want men rising up and leading their families. A house divided cannot stand.

Above everything else, Gary and I are friends. We have learned how to love each other, to meet each other's needs, but we are friends first. It started that way and keeps growing deeper as we walk through new seasons together, hand-in-hand and heart-to-heart. We don't always agree on everything, we don't always do what we should, but we each know that we are committed to always being there for each other.

Respect is a large part of our love. I respect the pressures upon him to provide, protect, lead, and love our family and me. He understands that I need reassurance of his love through verbal communication and time where he is focused on me and the family. I want the security of his love for life, and he needs to know that I am always there for him and I respect him. It's very comforting and reassuring to us both as we face outside pressures and dream about and create the future together. No ambition or desire takes the place of our first commitment to love each other.

We are committed to growing old together. The day before our wedding over thirty-three years ago, a note attached to yellow roses from Gary read, "Looking forward to spending the rest of my life with you." We have both shared this phrase back and forth since then. He has honored his commitment through all the ups and downs, and I respect him for it.

Gary always tells men their prosperity is limited by how well their marriage is functioning. Everything good, everything God wants to bring to pass, has to flow through that union. Peter warns that if a man doesn't walk with understanding with his wife, his prayers will be hindered (1 Peter 3:7). First Timothy 5:8 says, "Anyone who does not provide for their relatives, and especially for their own household, has denied the faith and is worse than an unbeliever." Marriage is important. Whatever starts at the top travels to the bottom—so what happens at the head of the family, the marriage, is going to affect the children and the family unit.

More than anything, men need respect from their wife. Typically, we meet someone we respect and think we would like to have their love and commitment, but once we have it, we tend to disrespect them if we don't get what we want. If we feel unloved by him, why not punish him with our words and by withholding sexual intimacy to show him how unhappy we are with him? This is very dangerous and is as good a way to destroy a marriage as if we had an outright affair. Men need to have a supportive friend in a wife who builds him up, believes in him, and foremost, respects him. Sometimes this process takes faith. The rewards of the Lord are about staying in the process! It's not always easy, but we're placing our trust not just in our mate, but also in God and His plan. The joys of inheriting the promises of God *together* are worth it.

When men don't receive respect, they lose hope in themselves. Grown men around the world need to hear the same message your mom once told you: "You can do better than this. I believe in you." What we need is a *"pro-men and pro-women working together"* movement in our culture. Unity is powerful.

Galatians 5:15 ESV warns, "If you continue hurting each other and tearing each other apart, be careful, or you will completely destroy each other."

Women need to feel esteemed as the most valuable thing in a man's life besides God. That's why in marriage, if a woman discerns that hunting, or baseball, or cars, or motorcycles, or something else seems to take preeminence over her relationship, her husband is going to have problems. Here's a little secret: the law of sowing and reaping works in marriage, too.

> No ambition or desire takes the place of our first commitment to love each other.

Women, if you show respect for your husband, he can rise to the occasion and lead your family. It might seem easier when you're younger to take charge of your family, pay the bills, and make the big decisions, but when you're older, you're going to want a husband whom you can lean on and who can take care of you. You have to allow your husband to become the leader he needs to be; don't take his place. You might be able to step into his role for a while, but eventually you and your family are going to need him to step up—and if you don't let him fill those shoes now, he won't know how when you need him to later.

Making mistakes is part of learning leadership. As women we shouldn't pretend to know it all and criticize our husbands as they try to lead. Over the last thirty years our society has so focused on encouraging women to lead that men have lost much of the confidence that was once a large part of their ego to protect women. It used to be called *chivalry*. When we watch the old movies, we love the guy who took care of the lady and treated her as a lady. Thankfully this has been restored in my marriage.

I'm not arguing against equality in pay or opportunities for women, but it's sad that today's women are worse off than ever in their relationship happiness. I'm not sure how warm and loving a briefcase and boardroom are when you're in your late sixties or seventies. I enjoy our business pursuits, but without my husband or family, they would be empty for sure!

I was recently playing with my granddaughters and grandson at the playground when three little Amish boys began to show me (and my granddaughters) all they could do—climbing, swinging high, then swinging in a standing position with smiles from ear to ear. It was such a cute display of how strong a young man feels when women admire them (at whatever age). Men want to perform for the respect and admiration of a woman unless something has stolen their spark.

Whether it's the emotional, financial, or communication skills to make a marriage work, or something else, most couples come into marriage missing something they need. God can supply what you need and train you in your marriage. If you and your spouse came into marriage missing a lot of things, or you let go of some things along the way—wisdom, maturity, humility, passion, communication—it's not too late to ask God to bring that into your marriage.

Do Your Life Together

Gary and I have a two-seater bike that we love to ride on our quaint country roads. Last spring, despite being repeatedly told we were crazy to try it as well as not being in great shape, we decided to take a hundred-mile tandem bicycle ride around Lake Tahoe, California. It was advertised as "America's Most Beautiful Bike Ride," and I pictured this really fun, daring, romantic day of adventure.

That's how you thought marriage was going to be, right? You think, *Oh, my spouse is going to bring me breakfast in bed. Oh, he's going to tell me how much he loves me every day. Life is going to be so fun and romantic. When we have children, they're going to be perfectly dressed and perfectly behaved.* And you don't think about the hundreds of diapers you'll be changing, or what it's going to be like when you have to bike up a seven-mile stretch of mountain road hitched with this other person to your bike.

My picture of Lake Tahoe couldn't have been further from the truth. Lake Tahoe was surrounded by daunting mountains! But wait, it gets worse. On the day before the bike ride, I was in line to register us and get our gear. The man standing in front of me turned around and asked the question I was dreading. "So, how long have you been training?"

I forced a smile. "Well, we haven't really been training," I admitted. I could almost feel the judgment seeping from the people around me who had been training for months upon months, and some for a year. "We've done twenty miles on our tandem bicycle."

"You're doing this on a tandem bicycle?" he asked, appalled. "And you're going to go a hundred miles tomorrow?"

"Yeah, my husband and I are doing it together."

> If you and your spouse came into marriage missing a lot of things, or you let go of some things along the way—wisdom, maturity, humility, passion, communication—it's not too late to ask God to bring that into your marriage.

"You're crazy!" he exclaimed. "You might as well throw in the towel right here! There's no way you're doing a hundred miles. I've been training and getting in shape for this, and I can only do the seventy-two-mile route."

I had to stand in line by that man for thirty minutes and listen to him tell me how there was no way Gary and I could accomplish this bike ride. He was much younger and more athletic than us, so it was intimidating. Luckily, when somebody tells me I can't do something, it only motivates me more. I committed to crossing that finish line, even if only to prove this man wrong.

When I finally got up to the registration table, the lady asked, "Are you sure the hundred-mile route is what you want to do?"

I had to decide if we were going to choose the harder road of success. The word was almost painful as it escaped my mouth. "Yes."

We started on the flat part of the ride, and it was fun and beautiful. It was just like life—you start out so good, so naive, so full of newlywed expectations. As we got farther into it, we started hitting some hills. And it started getting a little hard. As I watched the stretches of steep roads spreading far ahead of us, I realized how impossible coming back appeared. These sections were miles and miles long of nonstop climb. We were already tired, and we'd already gone much farther than we ever had before.

By the time we arrived at the lunch stop, Gary didn't want to eat. He was pale and spent. I could tell that he was getting too tired to go on, and we still had miles of mountain ahead of us. I went into my "prayer closet," which happened to be the portable potty there, and I began praying out loud, forgetting that I wasn't in the privacy of my home. I usually pace when I pray intensely, but in the portable potty, there was only room to sway back and forth as I pleaded, "God, please help us! Give us the grace to do this!"

I marched out of the portable potty, and the people around it stared at me. A man standing by said, "Are you all right?" I guess

I had been praying a little louder than I thought. I returned to Gary, determined to get us back on the road and to the finish line. I felt God's grace on me.

"I don't know, Drenda—" he mumbled weakly.

"Don't say anything. We're going to be fine."

I got him to stand up, then walk, then get back on the bike. Off we went again! We finally hit eighty-three miles. The only problem was that the next eleven miles were straight up the worst climb of the entire bike ride. We were so close to one hundred miles, yet so far away! But how could we stop so close to our dream?

Both of us were exhausted, Gary was dehydrated, and we struggled mentally to go on. He stretched out, resting and rehydrating, as I walked in circles keeping my legs moving and

> Life is better when we do life together.

trying not to lose faith. Then a male spectator insulted Gary by saying, "She must be the athlete in the family." In that moment I knew that though my man was down, he would rise to rescue me as he had done so many times, and it was my turn to help him finish his dream. So I did what we women know how to do best; I appealed to his manhood ever so gently, offering to push the bike up the hill and encouraging him to catch up with me when he was able. He immediately got up and joined me! Riding again, I told Gary how awesome he is (and he is!) and cheered him, and we peddled as never before. I kept saying, "Once we get to the top of this hill, we will coast almost the entire way to the finish line." I prayed for wind, for anything to help us make those last five miles when all had looked lost.

When we reached the mountain top, a surge of joy hit us both, and we flew down faster than I could imagine, going forty-five miles an hour on curvy mountainous drops. I closed my eyes, trusted my husband to steer, and prayed even harder, but I wasn't about to tell this man to slow down after what he had done!

We finished that race. We passed many of the cyclists who had taunted us, because we had more momentum going downhill with two on one bike. And we crossed the finish line to cowbells and shouts, and our family was waiting for us, cheering for us. That was a great moment for Gary and me. After we crossed the finish line, we hugged each other and broke into tears. We embraced, and I could feel our hearts beating as one. We were so proud of each other. We'd worked as a team and accomplished something that seemed impossible, and we also finished ahead of many of the naysayers who had passed us as we struggled on mile eighty-three.

It was much like the journey we have traveled together over life . . . a naive couple takes on a family, the dreams, the struggles, the disappointments, the challenges, the love, the encouragement, the teamwork, the deep respect and care for each other because of the many miles traveled as one.

Life is better when we do life together.

At the finish line of America's Most Beautiful Bike Ride.

Do you have a dream of something you would like to accomplish together with your spouse? What is it?

....
....
....
....
....

Do you think the culture portrays marriage with a healthy perspective? Why?

....
....
....
....
....

How can you help your spouse accomplish their dreams?

....
....
....
....
....

The Bible says that a man's prosperity is limited by how well his marriage is functioning. How do you think the marriage affects the rest of the family?

....
....
....
....
....

"The Good Wife"

FROM AN ANONYMOUS ARTICLE ABOUT THE 1950S

To be a good wife:

- Have dinner ready. Plan ahead, even the night before, to have a delicious meal ready on time for his return. This is a way of letting him know that you've been thinking about him and are concerned about his needs. Most men are hungry when they come home, and the prospect of a good meal (especially his favorite dish) is part of the warm welcome needed.

- Prepare yourself. Take fifteen minutes to rest so you'll be refreshed when he arrives. Touch up your makeup, put a ribbon in your hair and be fresh-looking. He has just been with a lot of work-weary people.

- Be a little gay and a little more interesting for him. His boring day may need a lift and one of your duties is to provide it.

- Clear away the clutter. Make one last trip through the main part of the house just before your husband arrives. Run a dust cloth over the tables.

- Over the cooler months of the year, you should prepare and light a fire for him to unwind by. Your husband will feel he has reached a haven of rest and order, and it will give you a lift, too. After all, catering for his comfort will provide you with immense personal satisfaction.

- Minimize all noise. At the time of his arrival, eliminate all noise of the washer, dryer, or vacuum. Encourage the children to be quiet.

- Be happy to see him. Greet him with a warm smile and show sincerity in your desire to please him.

- Listen to him. You may have a dozen important things to tell him, but the moment of his arrival is not the time. Let him talk first—remember, his topics of conversation are more important than yours.

- Make the evening his. Never complain if he comes home late or goes out to dinner or other places of entertainment without you. Instead, try to understand his world of strain and pressure and his very real need to be at home and relax.

- Your goal: To try and make sure your home is a place of peace, order, and tranquility where your husband can renew himself in body and spirit.

- Don't greet him with complaints and problems.

- Make him comfortable. Have him lean back in a comfortable chair or have him lie down in the bedroom. Have a cool or warm drink ready for him.

- Arrange his pillow and offer to take off his shoes. Speak in a low, soothing pleasant voice.

- Don't ask him questions about his actions or question his judgment or integrity. Remember, he is the master of the house and as such will always exercise his will with fairness and truthfulness. You have no right to question him.

- A good wife always knows her place.

"The Modern Good Wife"

According to the modern woman who found the '50s version distasteful:

- Be sure he has good, easy-to-follow directions to the quality restaurants that deliver curbside. This way when he arrives home, he'll have exactly what he wants for dinner, it will be ready when he arrives, and you get fed, too. You can be a dear and call in the order. We know how he doesn't like to do that.

- Prepare yourself . . . a good cocktail will work.

- Be a little gay (we now know this means happy). The cocktail will relax you, and you'll appear to be happy when he arrives.

- Clear away the clutter. Turn the computer off and turn the TV on, and kick stuff out of the way to make a straight path to the TV. That's all he'll notice.

- Be happy to see him. This may take several cocktails.

- Greet him with a warm smile and show sincerity in your desire to please him . . . more cocktails.

- Listen to him. This should be getting easy after several cocktails.

- He's coming home with a great dinner, and if he's late, make sure he knows how to use the microwave to reheat it. If he really comes home late and without dinner, have your dinner delivered and eat without him (just be sure he pays for your dinner when he does get home). No need to try to understand his world of strain, because you were out there all day, too.

The contrast from 1955 to today is pretty astonishing! Although as a modern woman you can obviously see things in the '50s model that you find controversial, notice the honor for a position of leadership and provision that a wife was to give to her husband? And although you and I may not agree with everything, the sharp contrast between that era and today's total disrespect for husbands, the modern-day woman boasts, may be one of the reasons we see the marriage and family breakdown.

I love getting to share life, family, ministry and business with this man!

Enjoying sodas on family night.

A Conversation Piece

COMMUNICATING TO SOLVE THE PROBLEM

"A happy marriage is the union of two good forgivers."

ROBERT QUILLEN

One day as our family was getting ready to go on a road trip, Gary and I had a disagreement. We drove from Ohio to Tennessee, a six-hour drive, and barely said a word. Sound familiar?

Strife is dangerous stuff. Whether it's between you and your spouse or you and your child, you do not want to let strife remain in your household. We knew it wasn't good, but neither of us wanted to let our pride down. I kept hearing the voice of the Lord, and I'd say, "No, I'm not going to fix this thing, because then I'd have to talk to him." It was almost a competition to see who could hold our grudge for the longest!

We drove farther and passed a car accident with children involved. One of their stuffed toys lay in the road. The Lord spoke to me, "Okay, this is your last warning. Are you going to continue this? You know you are opening the door to the enemy." Gary and I both felt the same conviction, but we pushed past it.

About an hour later, a car pulled out in front of our vehicle and without warning we were in what could have been a serious car accident. I started yelling the name of Jesus, and God supernaturally protected our entire family. Later, when I was recounting what happened, I said to someone, "I said the name of Jesus probably five or six times," and then realized that there were five people in the car. The name of Jesus covered every person in the car!

Initially, it looked as though there were going to be serious issues. They told us our son's spleen might rupture. I was pregnant, and the doctors worried that I might lose the baby. Through all these things we stood on the Word of God, and we came out unharmed, including the young preacher's son who pulled out in front of us and was in rebellion at that moment. And even in the midst of this difficult situation, through our prayers, standing on God's Word, and our children's words to the medical personnel, we had opportunities to minister and impact the little county hospital. The enemy set all of us up and tried to take us out, but the enemy lost the battle!

Nevertheless, there were consequences for our strife and disobedience. Gary and I had a small argument that escalated unchecked. The Bible says that where there is strife, there is confusion and there is every evil work (James 3:16). We were responsible for opening the door to the enemy, but the name of Jesus is more powerful than our circumstances and mistakes, and that is what kept us protected. The battle in your mind can change whether a situation ends in life or death. When you're put in a situation that tries to speak contrary to God's Word, what rises out of your spirit in that moment makes the difference.

Situations may catch you off guard, but God is never surprised.

He has already made a way for you and orchestrated it in your favor. You have to keep your eyes on the Word of God and keep a guard against strife, otherwise when the storms come, you're going to turn your eyes to the wrong thing.

Communication Styles

Communication is crucial with your children, in your marriage, and honestly, in every aspect of your life. When you have communication, you're going to have conflict. There are probably topics that you and your spouse or you and your child avoid. You know that if you talk about that, you will end up in an argument or in silence. What you may not realize is that the place that you cut off communication is the place that is holding you back. It's crucial that you learn how to do conflict resolution and stay in the will of God.

As we move forward, I will correlate these tactics to a spouse relationship, but these principles apply to any kind of conflict—business, friendships, and the one between you and your child.

What type of communication pattern do you fall under?

The Surrenderer

This person will avoid conflict at any cost, which usually means consenting to whatever their spouse says and shutting down the conversation as quickly as possible. They smile and reply, "Whatever, dear, whatever. It's okay. I don't even care about that anymore." They just want things to be happy, and the easiest way to do that is to ignore the problems. They do not share their feelings effectively.

My husband says about himself, "I'm a surrenderer, but I don't surrender easy!"

The problem with this communication type is that although they don't say anything, they harbor resentment from that conflict inside, and eventually it will spill out. They sacrifice expression to avoid conflict. Their spouse will also resent them for not caring enough about the relationship to talk things out.

The Withdrawer

This person pulls away from conflict and refuses to communicate. Instead of giving up and giving in as the surrenderer does, this person pulls away and shuts off. They give their spouse the silent treatment to avoid confronting the problem. This communication type is often manipulative. They don't want to discuss their feelings, but they silently view themselves as right and the victim in the situation. They tend to fall into the controlling and self-righteous category, which makes their spouse feel insecure and abandoned.

The Fighter

This person leads the argument and bulldozes over their spouse's feelings. They keep pushing their point, saying it in a different way, and going around the topic until their spouse surrenders. They're not just a fighter; they fight to win.

When two fighters are married, small discussions can turn into fireworks, because neither one will relent their point until they're the victor. Fighters are also easily irritated with people who withdraw or surrender in arguments, because they enjoy the confrontation.

I am a fighter. I have to make an extra effort to let Gary say what's on his mind when we're having a discussion, because otherwise he gives up on the conversation and surrenders. One time he said to me, "Drenda, I can never win an argument with you, because you have more words than I do. You're always going to come back with a new angle." This communication style causes others to feel unimportant, suppressed, and ultimately resentful.

Which one of these flawed communication systems do you lean toward? Which one does your spouse?

If you've been married for very long, you know how a discussion with your spouse is going to play out, don't you? If you're a fighter, you know when your spouse is going to finally withdraw or surrender. You count on the fact that if you can talk long enough, or go far enough, you'll get what you want out of the conversation. Nobody wins that way, though. Nobody wins with any of these confrontation tactics.

> You have to keep your eyes on the Word of God and keep a guard against strife, otherwise when the storms come, you're going to turn your eyes to the wrong thing.

We use these same communication styles in parenting our children, which is why we don't often get very far. Because Gary and I travel frequently, we observe parental dysfunction all the time in airports and on planes. For instance, as one of our flights was getting ready to taxi out for takeoff, suddenly two-year-old Bentley began kicking my seat from behind.

His mother is a surrenderer, and as a result, her son controlled her. I heard her say, "Bentley, stop that." The kicking did not stop, then again, "Bentley, stop that. There's a person in that seat, and we don't know who it is." Well, they may not have known who I was, but I knew who Bentley was.

Next, Bentley started the fake crying routine! Screaming, crying, and making the point that he was in charge.

Mom calmly said, "Bentley, stop that."

Bentley screamed, "No! No! No!"

"Bentley," she said, "stop that. Be quiet."

Bentley picked up the volume a few notches, and the now desperate mother pleaded, "Bentley, do you want some candy?"

When Bentley paid no attention to her offer, the flight attendant came quickly down the aisle and offered young Bentley a cookie. Miraculously, Bentley stopped screaming, said yes, and actually started laughing with his first bite.

His mom said, "Oh good, he likes it."

As I sat there, I couldn't believe what I was hearing. He likes it? Bentley did not need a negotiator; he needed a parent. All she needed to say was "Be quiet." Then when he started his screaming performance to protest, she could have taken him to the bathroom for a spanking, or if that was impossible, she could have done what Gary did on rare occasions with our children when we were out in public—he would reach over and give them a quick pinch on the back of the leg. I didn't necessarily like it, but it worked! We could take our children anywhere and they behaved.

> We use these same communication styles in parenting our children, which is why we don't often get very far.

Gary would have then said, calmly, "Bentley, I said stop." If Bentley still persisted, another pinch would have reinforced his authority, and he would have calmly repeated his command. It would not have taken too many pinches for little Bentley to know that he could not act that way. Children often use the public setting to assert rebellion because they feel they can. This becomes a pattern he will repeat!

The mother's surrender only made Bentley more demanding and more difficult to handle. The surrendering communication style is one of the communication styles learned after the Fall in the garden. Some parents withdraw, not speaking to their children for days, and others fight and are verbally and sometimes physically abusive. However, we don't have to communicate using any of these destructive methods. It's our choice. We can team up with God and step into a new kind of communication and love, and that kind can radically transform our relationships.

The Goal Is Agape

Agape commitment is unconditional. It says, "We made a vow to stay in this marriage. We're committed to communicating, so we're going to stay here until we come to a resolution. We made a commitment to train our children in the way they should go, not to let them destroy their life and future by becoming a demanding self-centered person." That is commitment. That is the reason to work through communication with your spouse. That is the reason to teach your children self-control and manners through discipline.

Love is not an emotion; it's an action. It's a commitment to sacrifice selfishness for what's best for the other person, whether they realize it or not. The Bible paints a portrait of this love and its characteristics. This must become our communication style: "Love is patient, love is kind. It does not envy, it does not boast, it is not proud. It does not dishonor others, it is not self-seeking, it is not easily angered, it keeps no record of wrongs. Love does not delight in evil but rejoices with the truth. It always protects, always trusts, always hopes, always perseveres" (1 Corinthians 13:4–7).

So how should you communicate?

- You shouldn't keep a record of your spouse's wrongdoings and bring them up in arguments.
- You should be patient with your spouse.

- You should not boast about yourself or be self-righteous and prideful.
- You should not dishonor your spouse.
- You should not get easily angered.
- You should rejoice with the truth.
- You should protect your spouse.
- You should trust your spouse.
- You should hope for the best in your spouse.
- You should persevere through obstacles.

Communication is a life-and-death situation to relationships. So in love, we can't surrender and just give in all of the time (more like give up on communication), we can't withdraw and cut off communication, and we can't bulldoze people out of our life.

Most conflict, according to the Word of God, is born out of selfishness. "What causes fights and quarrels among you? Don't they come from your desires that battle within you? You desire but do not have, so you kill. You covet but you cannot get what you want, so you quarrel and fight. You do not have because you do not ask God. When you ask, you do not receive, because you ask with wrong motives, that you may spend what you get on your pleasures" (James 4:1–3).

When we are born again in Christ, we have a new nature. Before we know God, it is fight to win, because that's the only escape out of the earth-cursed system. We strive to win, take care of ourselves, and provide for ourselves by putting self before others. Once we're born again, that changes. Empathy begins to take place. God begins to give you compassion, and you care for other people. God softens your heart.

Before Gary's father was saved, he showed little affection. He grew up in the "John Wayne era" when real men weren't supposed to show emotion, so he didn't tell his sons that he loved them. When he got saved at the age of eighty, he had a complete heart change. You couldn't talk to him without him expressing his love for you!

When the apostle Paul wrote about lawsuits in the church, note this key phrase: "The very fact that you have lawsuits among you means you have been completely defeated already. Why not rather be wronged? Why not rather be cheated?" (1 Corinthians 6:7).

Paul states that to take a disagreement to the point of argument means that you have already been defeated. The issue is not whatever the quarrel is about; the issue is that you've stepped out of God's jurisdiction and are open to all disorder, all confusion, and every evil work. That is why Satan wants to get you in strife! Satan wants to rob you blind. He wants to steal from you and dishonor you, and he doesn't want you to enjoy God's Kingdom.

> In love, we can't surrender and just give in all of the time (more like give up on communication), we can't withdraw and cut off communication, and we can't bulldoze people out of our life.

Early in our marriage, when Gary and I were broke and living in chaos, we had to learn that there's no place for strife in our home. When we would start to get into an argument, we would stop, look at each other, and say, "I'd rather prosper." Recognize strife and stop it before it robs you.

You might say, "Well, I can't help it. It's impossible to keep strife out." But the good news is that you can! You don't have to enter into strife. Strife is not an automatic default setting for you. It's a reaction! It's how you've trained yourself to protect your emotions and handle conflict. If you're about to start a conflict, it's better to take a moment to calm down and then come back and talk about it. There is nothing good that comes out of strife. Besides the emotional turmoil of strife, there is also the spiritual door that opens to the enemy. The devil actually sets up doorways for strife, such as obstacles or difficult people crossing your path when you're tired, so he can have access to your life and hinder God's plan for you. You need to understand that strife is your enemy.

Satan is after the power of agreement, especially among spouses. He knows that if you stand in agreement with the Word of God, then His Word is going to produce every single time. That's why Satan has snares, tactics, pressures, and persecutions to move you off the Word of God. Strife opens the door, pulls us outside of the legal jurisdiction of the Kingdom of God, short-circuits the system, and cuts off God's ability to bring His Word to pass for us. It's as though we're floating in an ocean with no sail or forward momentum.

The Lord Must Build the House

Early on in our marriage I got a taste of vintage living, moving our family into an abandoned 1800s farmhouse. With its wide slat wooden floors, built in bookshelves, mature trees, and fragrant shrubs, it was charming in so many ways, much like the vintage approach to life. But it had its difficulties, too! It had vines that made their way through windows that no longer shut, a scary cellar with ancient creepy crawly bugs and rats and raccoons and ancient appliances. The worst situation was that our family of six shared one bathroom! Talk about vintage! Everyone had to wait his or her turn.

Families used to share, whether it was one car or one bathroom. I think it made them, and us, more closely knit together, creating a need for communication, cooperation, and consideration—three vintage values families need more of today!

In the beginning, it seemed like fun and adventure, but eventually I had to place a sign in the bathroom that said, "Make the

Choice to Rejoice," to keep myself from going in there to cry. There were some very tough times living there, and yet we made some of the most wonderful treasured memories I possess today. I had to make the decision to be happy following God's plan for our lives regardless of the challenges. God taught us rich lessons on love and communicating. We learned how to follow God and His Word while going through our own wilderness experience. We learned how to stop the strife and build a strong family bond and a life of faith, and that's what truly makes a house a home.

What started out as a plan to live there three years turned into almost nine, but eventually our family needed a modern new house, and we knew the only way to move from the old to the new was to exercise faith in God's promises. In Jeremiah 6:16 NET, the Lord says, "You are standing at the crossroads so consider your path. Ask where the old, reliable paths are [the vintage paths]. Ask where the path is that leads to blessing, and follow it. If you do, you will find rest for your souls." That rest is the rest of faith, believing in Him.

Gary and I made a list of the things we wanted to have in a home and land. Gary's list included 50+ acres, woods, a pond or wetland, and barn. I wanted a five-bedroom house for our large family and eventually a swimming pool. After agreeing together, praying over our list, and giving finances to underwrite a marriage conference to help families (our seed), a couple called and told us about 55 acres for sale. God literally led us to our property, which had everything on our list, including a barn!

While in the farmhouse, we paid off our debts and saved $50,000, but we knew our damaged credit history would require paying cash for the land. God brought an unprecedented bonus check of almost $30,000 to our business that month, and over the next two months, we received the remainder, paying cash at closing.

The answers to prayer about building our new home remain one of the greatest demonstrations of faith I have walked out. I read a book about being your own general contractor, and God directed our steps toward the right builder to frame our home and weather it in, and I would take care of subcontracting the rest. Meanwhile Gary attended to our business and new church.

We were slated to build in the spring, but I had this intense desire to have it framed in before winter. With just a few weeks to secure the house plan and make changes, we broke ground in the fall and got it under roof. The day they dug the basement, our family stood with excitement and amazement that our basement was bigger than the farmhouse. We cried and shook to actually see the object of our faith being raised day by day.

Paying cash as we built all winter long was a weekly step of faith, with many close calls and deadlines, but God always came through. Items that were on my wish list would show up in returns or clearances. Our children were part of the house of faith God built, assisting me, learning new skills, and rejoicing in the process. The children even wrote scriptures on wall studs. My eighteen-month-old was often covered in drywall dust, but we did it as a family!

When spring rolled around, we were given notice that we had to move out of the farmhouse by July 4! I was grateful for the direction by God's Spirit to build in the fall. We moved into our almost completed house on July 4, the Keesee family independence day, and finished the final details the next months while living there. God brought the picture of faith to pass as we believed, prayed, and spoke God's Word daily over every detail.

Families need homes, but more importantly they need the Lord to build the house or they labor in vain. Build a house of faith and boldly believe His Word. To a modern-day world, it may seem like an ancient path, but that's the path that leads to blessing and peace.

Walking on Words

In Matthew 14 is the famous story of Jesus walking on the water. The disciples saw Him coming out to them on the lake, and they thought He was a ghost. Peter called out to Jesus, "Lord, if it's you, tell me to come to you on the water." Jesus said, "Come." And Peter walked out on the water.

What's important to note is that Peter didn't walk on the water until Jesus spoke. He knew he couldn't walk on the water, but if Jesus said to walk on the water, he could walk on the words of Jesus. But as soon as Peter lost sight of that Word, the water became the water again. He saw the waves and felt the wind, and he got scared and started to sink. When Peter turned from the Word of God and put his focus on his circumstances, he couldn't walk on the water.

> The answers to prayer about building our new home remain one of the greatest demonstrations of faith I have walked out.

Have you ever acted on a word from God? Maybe God told you to get a new job or to move to a new state, and at first everything was exciting. You were walking on the Word fearlessly, because you knew what God had told you. And then, one day you forgot it. In a day's time your job and your house were no longer the exciting thing that God had called you to—they were just jobs and houses. Suddenly the new coworkers and neighbors you wanted to minister to became annoying neighbors and coworkers whom you couldn't wait to get away from. Like Peter, you stepped away from the Word of God—and you ended up in the water.

Satan wants to get your attention off the Word of God and back on your circumstances. He wants you to sink. All things are possible to those who believe, but if Satan can get you off of agreement with God's Word, the power of God is cut off from your life. When you are receiving the harvest, life is going to go better for your family. You won't have as much strife when the bills are being paid and your needs are being met. Gary and I started to receive God's blessing in our life when we protected our family from strife. If a tire blew, we didn't have to go dig through our couch cushions to find enough change to fix it. Life was fun again.

When you talk, you are releasing power into your situation. "The tongue can bring death or life; those who love to talk will reap the consequences" (Proverbs 18:21 NLT). Now, that can work in your favor, but if you aren't using your words wisely, it can cause you a lot of troubles down the road.

When some people pray, their perspective is that it's like writing a letter of requests to Santa Claus! People don't realize that God already gave them the keys of the Kingdom, and they are *always* releasing the Kingdom through their *words.* "Truly I tell you, whatever you bind on earth will be bound in heaven, and whatever you loose on earth will be loosed in heaven" (Matthew 18:18).

Wow! Whatever *you* bind on earth will be bound in heaven. That means that you directly control the blessing in your life. That gives a whole new revelation to the power of your words. So if blessing is being short-circuited in your life, guess who is binding that blessing? And if unfortunate circumstances are overrunning your life, guess who is loosing permission for Satan to attack?

You!

So when you tell your husband, "You *always* mess this up," you are loosing that over him. In other words, you are cursing him. The law of releasing life or death in your life is in the power of your tongue, and it is operating all the time. Your words are a weapon.

The Power of Oneness

"When we put bits into the mouths of horses to make them obey us, we can turn the whole animal. Or take ships as an example. Although they are so large and are driven by strong winds, they are steered by a very small rudder wherever the pilot wants to go. Likewise, the tongue is a small part of the body, but it makes great boasts. Consider what a great forest is set on fire by a small spark" (James 3:3–5).

> The law of releasing life or death in your life is in the power of your tongue, and it is operating all the time.

I encounter so many Christians who don't understand how they could aim for somewhere great in life and still end up shipwrecked. It's because they set in motion the law to go there. They wanted to end up prosperous and successful, but they spoke poor words over their lives. Your words are the rudder for your life, and they steer you toward your future. Even when there is wind pushing against the boat, your words can steer you toward your goal, and they can steer your marriage and family toward safety.

When you begin to understand the laws working behind strife, you see how it is detrimental to your life. We should constantly examine our words and make sure they are steering us in the right direction. Satan does not want your mouth to be in agreement with heaven. The Bible says if you speak it and believe it in your heart, you can move mountains (Mark 11:23). Satan doesn't want mountains moved. He doesn't want to lose territory. He doesn't want to see your family whole.

You may say, "Well, my family knows what we're believing for." Really? Check out your words. If your words don't line up with what you believe, you aren't going to receive it. When you're tempted to fall into strife, you need to say, "Let the winds and waves blow against us, but we're not changing course."

Communication is a vital part of walking in unity. You have to talk about things with your spouse and family, and the good news is you can do it without strife! If there is a topic that a husband and wife don't talk about because it's a sore spot, Satan can throw that up to you whenever he wants to get you in strife. You need to talk out those sore spots and put an end to them once and for all.

The Bible says you're one with your spouse. It's not about you anymore. It's about the two of you, and the sooner you learn to communicate and come to an agreement with each other, things are going to begin to flow in your life and in your family life.

Jesus cursed a fig tree and caused it to die with His words (Matthew 21). The law of words works both ways. Be careful not to curse the people in your life. I cringe when I hear mothers make statements such as, "Well, you're just a brat. You'll never amount to anything." They're releasing the power of their words into that situation, and it's going to lock that thing in place and hinder the child's ability to see past it. The Bible says we speak blessings and curses (James 3:10). Even the world's philosophies recognize this principle as a "self-fulfilling prophesy." What you speak to your family member derives an expectation that they either rise to or fall with. Words of encouragement are crucial to strong families.

Communication and understanding are crucial to this process. Gary loves to go deer hunting, and at the beginning of our marriage, I resented that. At the time, we were living in the farmhouse and I thought, *Why is he leaving me here to go hunting when there are so many things to get done?* Meanwhile, Gary is thinking, *I need a break. Why does she always have things for me to do when I want to go hunting?*

This is how the enemy divides us as husband and wife. He gets you looking at your needs, your issues, and your problems. And now we're pitted against each other instead of being in unity and working together against the enemy. As long as the enemy can divide us, he can conquer our family. He can come after our godly seed. He's after your kids, he's after your power, and he's after your authority.

Gary and I had to learn to understand each other. I knew hunting was important to him because God created men with the desire to provide for their family. And Gary had to learn to put our family and me first. When we learned to understand where the other person was coming from, we began to communicate better. I stopped using "you always, you never," because those words stop communication. They're judgmental words. I also had to learn to be honest when I was upset about something rather than harbor it. I've heard the expression that women are like volcanoes—they have to let off small eruptions or they explode!

When Gary and I were coming into agreement with each other, he would ask me, "Is there anything that would keep you from coming into agreement with me? Is there anything we need to talk out? Is there anything I can do to help you out?" That consideration diffused any negative feelings I would have about him going deer hunting. A woman is a responder. What her husband sows into her, he is going to reap.

When you start working together instead of working against each other, that's powerful. When you start communicating with understanding instead of with pointing and shouting, that's life-changing. The greatest area of agreement is between a husband and a wife. That's why Satan attacks marriages. He wants to keep couples so at odds that they can't come into agreement.

Before we took our children to Europe, Gary and I believed for a trip to Europe for ourselves. One of our company's vendors was offering a trip to Europe for those who met a certain amount of production for that year. It didn't look as though we were going to get the trip, but the agreement we came into almost a year prior to that was so strong that there was something in my spirit and my mouth that would not let me say we weren't going. Even when the deadline passed and we didn't have the production in our company to get the trip to Europe, I still believed we were going. A month went by, and we never said we didn't win the trip. Then one morning we received a phone call from our regional sales director.

> This is how the enemy divides us as husband and wife. He gets you looking at your needs, your issues, and your problems.

"Gary, the corporate office just called us," he said, "and they said they have two couples positions open on this trip. They're going to let you go since you were so close, and I get to go since I'm your RSD, even though we didn't qualify for the trip. Your prayers did this!"

We had told him that our faith was out for this trip, so he recognized the work of God in what had happened. Faith by example, remember? But it didn't stop there.

"And," he said, "my wife and I are so excited that we get to go, we want to pay for you both to go to Scotland with us before we go to London. How does that sound?"

"That sounds great!" Gary exclaimed.

The greatest part was that we got to use this time to connect with our regional sales director and his wife and eventually pray for them to receive the Holy Spirit! Gary and I could have gotten mad at each other and pushed blame when we didn't get the trip at first. I could have said if he wouldn't have jogged or hunted so much, we could have won the trip. If we'd done that, we wouldn't have gotten the trip. The power was in our agreement! When you walk in unity, everything else will flow—provision, promotion, and health. It's wonderful!

Prayer

As a husband and wife, you have to come to the place of unity. It may take some time and some work, but it's worth it. Changes in your family are going to start from the head down—from you, from your marriage, and then to your children and family unit.

I encourage you to release God's power and love into your marriage. Trust God and turn your situation over to Him. Please meditate on the words of this prayer. Pray them out loud and personally commit to uphold unity in your marriage.

> *Father, I thank You for my marriage and for my spouse. I thank You for unity even in hard times, and I pray that You bless our marriage. I come into agreement with my spouse, and I release Your power into our situation.*
>
> *I thank You that we learn to love like You do and we communicate with understanding.*
>
> *In Jesus' name, Amen!*

Which communication pattern do you lean toward? Which one does your spouse?

....

....

....

....

....

What are some communication habits you have in conflict and confrontation that you can improve in?

....

....

....

....

....

When Satan comes to steal the Word from you, how can you guard your heart and mind?

....

....

....

....

....

....

Do you feel that you're putting the power of agreement into action in your life? Why or why not?

....

....

....

....

....

Gary's
❯❯ MONOGRAPH ❮❮

HUSBAND, FATHER TO OUR FIVE CHILDREN

I thought now would be a good time to talk to the dads. Men, we have a "husband/father" crisis in America today. The world is a scary place, and many men have not been mentored to lead, let alone love their wives. I admit that I was almost clueless when it came to marriage and being a father. I was very insecure in my high school years with a 1.3 grade point average, and I wasn't voted the most likely to succeed. Drenda, on the other hand, was voted the most likely to succeed. She was a great leader, president of her high school class of 500+, editor of the school paper, a successful sales person, and a 4.0 student. It did not require a counselor to predict there would be some conflict when we got married. I had a lot to learn.

In our thirteenth year of marriage, we launched a church and decided to do a marriage conference as an outreach to our community. As I started thinking about doing this conference, I asked Drenda, "How can I do a marriage conference? I don't know anything about marriage."

She looked me in the eye with a slight smirk and said, "I know, that is why I suggested we do a marriage conference." I am still learning after thirty-four years of marriage, but I can tell you that your greatest asset in life is your marriage. Your wife is full of wisdom, and if you will love her and let her flow in her gifting, she will do you well all the days of your life.

We men easily get distracted, and unlike our wives, we're not great at multitasking. If your wife decides to clean the bedroom, for instance, you can bet that you'll later find her digging through a drawer or the closet, trying to figure out where every little piece of something goes. And you probably hear your wife state that you can clean house much faster than she does. That is because she is made to multitask with great detail, which complements her role of being a mom plus doing a thousand things on the side.

But that also means there are a lot of things we men mean to do at home and for our wives, but we forget, right? It's easy to take our wives and our families for granted, not because we mean to, but we tend to focus on what has our attention at the moment. God designed us to focus for a reason. We are designed to be out in the world protecting and providing for our families. We are designed to be put in some very stressful emotional situations and stay focused. So may I suggest that you stay focused on your wife—the Lord first, then your wife, then your children. I needed help with this and still do—all of us men do. I would suggest that you go as far as to schedule your appointments with your wife each week and make her a priority! It will go well with you, trust me.

It did not always go well with me. Drenda and I had tons of debt, with no hope of being able to pay it back in the early days. Living paycheck to paycheck wasn't enough, and the debt kept growing. IRS liens, tens of thousands of dollars owed to relatives, canceled credit cards, car loans, judgments, and liens all faced me each day. Being in sales, I worked nonstop under great anxiousness and fear all week long, including Saturday, trying to survive the financial week, usually with dismal results.

Through this period of time I withdrew from my family into my own little world of stress and had no time for communication with my wife or being a father to my children. Unfortunately, this lasted for a few years. Our home movies from that period are so sad. In one movie my family is all outside waiting for me to pull in. I pull up and get out of the car, and all my beautiful little children let out a squeal as they scream, "Daddy's home!" and come running. In the film I say nothing to them. I do not acknowledge them, do not look at them, and walk straight into the house without saying anything to them or my wife. My face is blank, showing no emotion. I'd like to shake that fellow, wake him up, and make him look around at what he has. Fortunately, God has a way of getting our attention if we will only listen.

We had made the long drive to Drenda's parents' house for Father's Day. It was Sunday morning, and we were all going to church with her parents. It was time to leave, and Tom, my four-year-old, could not find his shoes—again! Tom could rarely find his shoes any time we went somewhere. We looked and looked but could not find them, which made us late, and I had had it. I was already stressed out with everything in life, and I lost it and began screaming at Tom, "Why can't you ever find your shoes? You always lose your shoes, and I am tired of it!" My four-year-old cowered before me in deep sobs. I felt justified in my anger as I felt I needed to teach this little guy a lesson. Just then Amy, my oldest daughter, cried out that she had found the shoes. We made a mad dash for the door and got in the van. As we were driving to church, Tom sat in the back of the van, crying silently with deep sobs. I paid no attention to him. When we got to church, we saw that the children's department was actually in a separate building. Amy offered to take the younger children with her, so Drenda and I went straight into the main service without talking to Tom as he left.

> You can be a great dad! God will help you. Why don't you stop right now and ask Him for His help. He will strengthen you and give you wisdom. I know He will; He did it for me!

It was Father's Day, and the pastor taught on what a godly father was. I sat there paralyzed by the conviction of the Holy Spirit, but it wasn't just about that one event. I was convicted on how I was treating my wife, my family, and even God. At the end of the service the pastor asked for those who wanted prayer to come forward. I was the first one down front, and now it was me who was weeping with deep sobs. I was grief stricken when I realized what I was doing to my family. Of course, my first order of business was to apologize to little Tom. As I walked out the church door, all the children were being released to go to their parents. A crowd of children was moving toward me, but I was only looking for one. The minute Tom spotted me, he ran full speed to me and immediately grabbed my leg and began to cry out, "I'm sorry I lost my shoes, Daddy!" He was sobbing again and repeated, "I'm sorry I lost my shoes, Daddy." It made me very sad to realize that he took all the blame for his daddy getting so upset.

I quickly picked him up, and we both wept together. "No, Tom, Daddy was wrong. Will you please forgive Daddy? I am sorry I was so upset with you." Tom looked at me with the tears still falling down his face and nodded his head yes. He then held out to me something that up until that moment I hadn't noticed. It was a piece of yellow construction paper with a drawing he had made during class. It was a picture of me holding a fishing pole and at the end of the line was a fish. The farmhouse we rented had a small pond that the boys and I would occasionally fish in, and this is what he had drawn. Across the top of the page he had written *yad srehtaf yppah* in big messy letters. My assumption is that the teacher had written Happy Father's Day on the board and he copied it backward for some reason. All of his letters were drawn backward as well. I didn't care; it meant the world to me. I cannot tell you how thrilled I was to hold Tom in my arms that day and to know that I had another chance to make things right.

That moment changed me. I've kept that yellow piece of paper all these years and from time to time, I look at it and let it remind me that relationships in my family are more important than anything else. It reminds me that I need God and that I cannot handle life on my own. I had many more lessons to learn during those years, and there were things I look back on that make me ashamed. But I am grateful that God let me see myself on that day before it was too late. I know other dads who did not find out what I found out until years after their children were grown and gone and there was no way to get those years back.

Until my father gave his heart to Christ at the age of eighty, he never once told me that he loved me. I cannot remember him telling my mother that he loved her and cannot remember him showing her affection. I'm sure this had a huge bearing on me not showing my emotion as well. Although my dad and I had a somewhat good relationship, I prayed that he would someday know Christ. When that finally happened, he was transformed before my very eyes. His first order of business was to repent to my mother and then to us kids, wanting all of us to know how much he loved us. For the next three and a half years, he made it his goal to tell me he loved me every time he saw me and to tell me how proud he was of me. He was a completely changed man. Right before he died, he told me how sad he was that he had wasted his life and that he had never told me that he loved me or shown his family love. Those three and a half years were a gift from God to me. But I think of how much my dad missed.

If I could say one thing to you, don't miss the moment. Time goes so fast, and you only have so much time to love and invest in your children. Although I had some rough days in the early part of being a dad, our family went on to being inseparable. We traveled the world together, and my family is my greatest joy. I look back now on those early days and cannot believe what I might have missed.

You can be a great dad! God will help you. Why don't you stop right now and ask Him for His help. He will strengthen you and give you wisdom. I know He will; He did it for me!

And by the way, the financial mess was fixed, and we went on to be debt free with God's help. We prospered beyond our wildest dreams. I now do a daily TV broadcast called *Fixing the Money Thing*, which reaches every time zone in the world. Crazy, isn't it? Who would have ever guessed? Let God show you how to change your life. He will make it into an amazing story!

Mompreneurs and Home Managers

CREATE A BALANCE

"The phrase 'working mother' is redundant."

JANE SELLMAN

With over half the workforce comprised by working moms, many women struggle with the balance of work and home life. What are the benefits of becoming a "mompreneur"? How can it work to help you build a marriage and family that recaptures a vintage approach to sharing developmental moments with your child? Whether you develop a business or not, these principles can guide your home and the "family-life business."

All five of our children are entrepreneurial, self-motivated, and highly torqued to create. How did they develop this way? By helping us in business and ministry! They caught our passions as children and learned as we did. So when mothers ask me, "Is it possible to have a successful business alongside my family?" my answer is a resounding yes! My goal here is to share the vision of the New Vintage family business and give you the basics to prioritize and build it, but regardless of whether you own a business, we all must balance home life with work. Seasons in life have different challenges, and you decide how to meet those challenges by determining what is the greatest priority in that season and how to balance family life with it. It's important to begin to build today for the life you want to have tomorrow, and this especially holds true in the family and a business enterprise.

Gary and I decided over thirty years ago that we would develop and manage a business as a husband and wife team. I would work at our business from home with our small children and growing family, and Gary would go on sales calls and manage the office. Of course, there was the question of whether we could afford one income stream, but we chose to make it work for the well-being of our children.

There were sacrifices Gary and I made, but the one sacrifice we were not willing to make was our children. Not having the best car and living in an 1800s farmhouse with one bathroom for a season were small sacrifices in comparison to being able to raise our children. You have to do what you need to do to make it work. I shopped in consignment stores, found bargains at garage sales, and did without some of the "things" my peers had acquired on debt. I chose that route so I could be with my family and pour my heart and resources into their development. Gary also made sacrifices, but what seemed like sacrifices to us then have become some of our fondest memories today. It's true that the journey is greater than the destination.

I was able to be a "stay-at-home mom," but in reality I was what is now called a "mompreneur." Gary and I decided to operate our own business and bring our individual skills and personalities together as a team to build it. Through the years, I could change business roles and time commitments to accommodate the needs of our family so that our primary focus—our family—could have the priority it deserved.

Early on, when our business was struggling to get off the ground, we had to take our family television (which I'm now grateful was absent from our home in the early childhood years) to the office so we could share company training and recruiting videos with our sales staff. A special treat for our two children, ages three and four at that time, was going to the office board-room and spending Friday night in their sleeping bags watch-ing Christian cartoons on VHS while Gary and I planned sales meetings, completed payroll, cleaned the offices, and organized papers. They would often fall asleep as we worked into the night to complete our tasks, which also allowed Gary and me to perform tasks we couldn't afford to hire staff to do.

> One of the benefits of combining home education with self-employment was that we had freedom.

We also went through two differ-ent seasons where we ran our business out of a section of our home. In these transitional times, it gave us the ability to run our operations completely from home, since our clients commonly met us in their home across the kitchen table. Once the children were down for naps or in bed for the evening, I was able to complete underwriting, client follow-up, and various strategy sessions with Gary. He was the "boots on the ground" force, meeting our clients face-to-face most evenings, but our teamwork was clearly always the mode of operating our business. Little did I know how much training we were getting for the ministry we would do in life's next chapter.

As time progressed, the rewards of having our own busi-ness from home became greater than I ever anticipated. Our daughters loved to borrow any leftover supplies and play office in our playroom. I involved our children in various tasks in the company. They could file, go with me to the copy shop to make sales brochures, banners, and newsletters. They "caught" an entrepreneurial spirit in the process, and the educational ben-efits were greater than a classroom.

I home educated our children, and one of the benefits of combining home education with self-employment was that we had freedom. Freedom gave us opportunities and an amazing lifestyle that set us apart from the normal eight to five, Monday to Friday, two weeks off a year, working class. We were able to go see the world with the freedom and finances that having our own business and educating our children eventually gave us.

When our finances were tight, our vacation travels were to visit national parks and camp along the way, but as our business and children grew, we took our children on mission trips across the world and visited Alaska, Hawaii, Europe, Mexico, Canada, and even remote places such as Albania or Corsica. Our children not only got a world-class education, but they experienced it as well! They learned how to navigate the Metro in Paris and to perform music and evangelistic dramas for families in outreach settings in Albania. And our business funded the trips with accrued credit card points, airline miles, and hotel points to boot!

The Vintage Way

I look back on those "pioneer days" as the best of times. Exploring new adventures with our kids by our side and building a company that has had a lasting impact on our family and other families has been a thrill to experience. I wouldn't do it any differently. I see our adult children now passionately working toward similar pursuits and goals, and I am eternally thankful we did life a different way than the norm.

I'm not saying everyone has to approach finances and family this way, but this was the American way in the early days of our nation. Entrepreneurship made up over 80 percent of all jobs. The rest of workers were apprenticed with the mindset of eventually owning their own business. Sadly, today those numbers are flipped.

Most people work for someone else with little freedom or potential to one day own their job. Many moms join the workforce and leave children to a school system run by the government. The impact on families has resulted in children who rarely see their parents and instead obtain their values, education, and direction from the state or federal government. The loss of the family business—a common family vision—is another factor contributing to the demise of family life.

Building a business is a learning process. It requires passion, dedication, growth, perseverance, and above all, character. This was the learning process that made America a great nation before our nation's priorities changed, forcing families apart. Character is a vintage value missing in our culture today.

How would you begin to build a family business, whether you want to accomplish it as your only income source or in addition to another family member's employment? The key to this decision is passion. *Mompreneur Magazine* recommends, "Investigate the types of businesses that offer the types of service that align with your passion. Set the intention to find a way to do what you really love to do. With the computer and telephone, the world is at your fingertips."

For us, our passion was to help families fund their God-given assignments and live a great life of financial freedom. Freedom to follow God's calling and vocation for your life trumps having "things" and losing sight of preparing your children for life. Don't get caught in a debt trap. If you have a vision that's greater than things, you can build real wealth in your children and finances at the same time.

Determine your passions. What problem can you solve? What area could you start to develop and learn? How could that become a business that serves your family and others? Where could you be apprenticed to learn and develop the "know how"? What impact would the business have on your family in the short and long term? What could various family members contribute to building it, and how could it help your children integrate and develop their passions into adulthood?

Looking back, we really didn't see all of the outcomes I am sharing with you in hindsight. Our passion to help families made it all worth it, and you have to believe that to ever take the first step (especially if you're starting out broke and in debt as we did!). But as I write today, I am sitting on the front porch of our paid-for home with sixty acres after just returning from a wonderful ministry trip to Japan with my daughter. My granddaughter is sleeping upstairs, and our youngest daughter is in her room editing chapters of this book for me. My husband is planning at the office of the financial services company we started thirty-four years ago. Our daily television programs are teaching other families to engage the Kingdom of God and manage their life and finances as we have learned from God's Word. All of this was homegrown from a seed of vision and love.

Our adult children are developing television programs, pastoring adults and children, writing worship music and recording albums, and building businesses. Our life feels very complete. Do we have challenges? Sure. But following God's plans for freedom and taking responsibility for our life is much more rewarding than renting our life out to a corporation and giving our children to the government to control.

Write the Vision

So how do you make this happen? First, write the vision by seeing the desired end, and then develop the pathway to get there.

Make a pathway that leads to your dream! Life is like a pathway with people trying to steer you throughout your journey to go where the masses go, to do what everyone else is doing in education, family, finances, food, fashion, and fun. There are those who are trying to capture your finances, your family, your time, and your influence. They have devised well-planned businesses to extract these things from you. They are getting you to hand over your power by luring you through your feelings. They use great enticements to create feelings that make you spend, make you want, make you lust. You spend; they cash in. Meanwhile, the schools are training your children to think and live by their moral code, which is sorely lacking in absolutes.

Make a written plan so you are *not* put on their pathway. Make your own pathway with God's direction and walk it out. The pathway is a plan. You were created to live by design, not by default! Start to plan instead of being one of the easily led masses that don't think or plan for their life.

If you have children at home, explore how your family can be a part of your pathway. How do you incorporate them? Mentor them for success? Apprentice them in biblical success principles, habits, and train them? I believe your business can be one of the best places. You may not be able to have a corporate job and take the kids to work, but you can build your own corporation with your family alongside.

There was a single woman in the Scriptures whose husband died and left her with a huge debt. The creditors were going to take her sons in exchange for the debt! It's what they did back then. But how is it much different today, if we let debt take parents from their children, who are working and slaving to pay back creditors? This woman sought God for answers by going to Elisha the prophet (2 Kings 4). The prophet told her to gather pots and "not a few." In other words, go into a big vision for your business!

She and her sons gathered the pots and began to pour the oil they had into the pots. God multiplied their efforts, and the oil didn't run out until all the pots were filled. She sold the oil, paying off her debt. The first recorded female entrepreneur started out as a broke, single mom, but became a mompreneur. I celebrate how God will fill the family business with His blessing as we expand our thinking and gather a harvest financially where He instructs us.

Mompreneur Success Story

Growing up, Sara wasn't interested in working in a traditional office environment. After her first experience in a business office, she asked her mom, "Why would anyone want to work for someone else? And why would anyone work in this type of environment? It's depressing!" She understood at an early age that she wanted something different for her life than the "nine-to-five employee" model.

> Write the vision by seeing the desired end, and then develop the pathway to get there. Make a pathway that leads to your dream!

Sara worked at a job over the next few years where she could set her own schedule, until one of the accountants at her job approached her and asked if she was interested in starting her own bookkeeping business. She raised an eyebrow, thought about it for a moment, then said, "Okay." She didn't know the first thing about what having her own business would entail, but she loved the idea of making a living from the comfort of her home.

She started processing tax returns for people who claimed bankruptcy. She took on bookkeeping clients from accounting firms and over the next two years her business grew to the point where she had employees working under her. Then her assistant decided she needed a full-time job that paid more and had benefits, leaving Sara to work long nights, not even sleeping for some, all to keep up with the workload. She was more and more absent from her two-year-old son and husband.

Then she had a revelation. Roger, her husband, always wanted to be a stay-at-home dad and also had a bookkeeping degree. So Sara asked him to quit his job. They made the transition from him working full time to both of them working at home. It didn't get easier for Roger and Sara, though. Clients came and went, and money wasn't coming in as they had hoped.

Over the next three years they refinanced their home twice and were spending more than their income. Sara says she felt like she was on a merry-go-round that was speeding up, and she was headed for the same place she had promised herself she'd never go—bankruptcy. But that's when something life-changing happened.

Roger turned on his television, and there was my husband, Gary, telling our story of financial struggle and how we overcame our overwhelming amounts of debts in two and a half years. Roger and Sara were blown away. They began to see a light at the end of the tunnel. They decided to purchase Gary's "Financial Revolution" teaching, but they didn't have the $35 to buy it! So they returned a lamp they had purchased to get the money, ordered the set, and Sara says, "It was one-hundred percent life-changing material. We changed our mindset and relationship concerning money, which finally got us off that merry-go-round!"

Three years later, after doing some research, Sara realized she was only charging one-third of the rate she was worth! She realized that she was robbing her family. She tripled her rate for new clients that were coming to her business, and guess what? The clients had no problem paying the new fees.

Sara says, "As women, we tend not to see our worth. We don't value our time and skills."

Today, Sara feels like she has the entire world in her hands. Their bookkeeping business is so successful that they've had to hire more employees, their family is happy, and they are now living in their dream home. Sara has won "20 Under 40" with *Business London Magazine* and Who's Who, Women in Ecommerce in North America. Sara says to women in her situation: "With the help of God, the tools He has placed inside of me, with the people I've chosen to surround myself with, and with my faith—I did it! And if you choose to allow God in, use the tools He has given you, surround yourself with the right people, and seriously have faith, then you *can* do it, too!"

Jesus' parents, Joseph and Mary, are the best examples of combining business with parenting. Jesus was mentored for success by His parents and in the synagogue. He was a carpenter in His father's business! I still think this is the most advantageous family design. He learned business as He learned His calling in the *nurture and admonition* of His parents. This was God's plan to raise Him and develop His character to reach His destiny. What home responsibilities will help mentor your child to succeed in life?

Our personal dream was to have a business that would fund the Kingdom of God and provide us with an income to accomplish the ministry God had for us. The apostle Paul was our example. He was a tentmaker who used his business as his means of support to reach people for Christ.

What's your personal dream? It must be bigger than paying bills or making money. Of course, we all want our ventures to be financially rewarding, but dreams are what motivate us when there's little to no financial compensation. If it's about money alone, you won't make it past the point when there's no money.

Life is more, and your destiny is greater. Your dreams must become goals with a pathway or strategy to get there.

Delete Distractions

Women are multitaskers, and that ability comes with pros and cons. The main hindering factor multitasking brings to the table is that it's easy to get distracted. We are fixers, always dropping what we should be doing for someone or something else. But flexibility shouldn't mean you're "always available." You should do personal favors outside of your scheduled work hours.

Unless you have a plan—a list of your priorities to do—you're planning to fail. Develop an action plan that has yearly, monthly, weekly, and daily must-dos. You need three to four things you do every single day that propel your business forward. I've found that it's not the amount of time you spend, but how you spend your time. Is it productive or wasted time? I want to tell you a secret that will transform how you work: *working* is the supreme driving force behind procrastination. That may sound like an oxymoron, but it's true. You can spend hours "working" and somehow manage not to check off one thing on your to-do list, because it's easy to use miscellaneous, unimportant tasks as an excuse not to work on high priority tasks. This is actually a biblical principle. Second Thessalonians 3:11 says, "We hear that some among you are idle and disruptive. *They are not busy; they are busybodies.*"

Time is your greatest asset. You must set boundaries around your time and relationships. If you attempt to solve everyone's problems and be available 24/7 to people, you will neglect your children and business. You can't do it all, so do what matters most. Break up with bad clients—the ones who cancel over and over, who require far more from you than the return. No amount of money is worth a client who doesn't respect you or your time. Break up with draining friendships that want to steal your future by their demands and intrusions. Real friends propel you toward your destiny and encourage you toward your dream instead of draining your energy and wasting your time. Surround yourself with people who make positive contributions to your life, and then you can reciprocate and encourage one another.

> Unless you have a plan—a list of your priorities to do—you're planning to fail.

Decide who and what you will give priority to in order to prevent burnout in your life. It's crucial that you set and honor work and life boundaries, especially if your business is run strictly out of your home. "Off" must mean "off." Set aside a family day, and let that be a day where you rest with your family and turn off the business side. Some of your best ideas and direction will come from the day you stop, trust God, and seek His rest.

By the same standard, "on" means "on." When it's time to work, discipline yourself to focus on the task ahead of you and get the job done, or you will sabotage your success and train those you love who are watching you to do the same. Remember: your time is your greatest asset. Protect it and use it wisely, or someone will take it from you. You don't want to look back with regret at the wasted time and lost opportunities you left scattered behind you. There is a time for everything, but is this the time?

Plan

It's crucial to have a well-planned strategy for your business before you go all in. Develop a business strategy for success that matches the goals and desires for your life. You and your family can brainstorm, research, and design all of the elements before you execute the plan, and that can make the startup a much smoother process. There are times to "test" concepts, but too many people enter entrepreneurship without a plan or understanding that it takes time to build a business. Oftentimes the best strategy is to test and build your business on a part-time basis before you dive into it full time and cash in your retirement savings to invest in the business. I can't emphasize how important it is to know your business and your customer well before you go all out. Who wants to buy your product or service? And even if it's a great idea, if you don't know how to execute it, it can still flop. Get your strategy and vision written and plainly defined.

Focus

Do what funds your business and fuels your family. As simple as this seems, what makes you money is getting your product or service before people. Gary and I have run a sales organization that we built from the ground up for over thirty years, which means we learned a lot the hard way. We had sales reps who blamed their performance on the size of the office or the supplies they had or our leadership, when the real issue was that they were choosing to do the wrong things. Shuffling papers when you should be seeing clients doesn't pay well. We had to redefine *work* as "when you're talking to a person, face-to-face, on the phone or computer, sharing your service or product." We limited the job description because it's easy to get distracted doing everything *except* what builds and funds the business. Activity that measures productivity and desired outcomes should be the focus of business and their employees. Certainly there are other functions in a business, but sales forces must be in front of people or there's no business. All business is sales in some form or fashion, whether you're offering a service or a product. What is your product and how will you take it to people? You can't wait for customers to find you, even if you operate a storefront.

Believe

There is also a belief factor. You must believe in what you're doing—that you can do it and should do it—or you will lack motivation. God and His Word have been our motivation—those are the promises and principles we live by. Many businesses do not operate with integrity and quickly gain a reputation for sloppy business practices or unethical dealings. You must keep your word and deliver your promise. The Book of Proverbs is full of sound advice, and I recommend reading one passage from the Proverbs every day to keep you on course.

My husband has wonderful resources on building businesses and getting out of debt, which I highly recommend. However, the most important knowledge or structure you need for your business is God and His Word. Let God and His principles exist as the foundation on which you build your business, or you labor in vain. When God speaks or you get ideas, write them down. Keep an idea journal. Don't let ideas escape—one of them might be the bridge to where you want to be tomorrow.

Persevere

Discouragement is the greatest enemy to any undertaking. "But you, take courage! Do not let your hands be weak, for your work shall be rewarded" (2 Chronicles 15:7 ESV). Stay with it until you finish it. Finish the project. Stick with the task. Are you listening to the voice that says you're a finisher, or are you listening to the accuser of the brethren? Your business will never be "done" or be perfect, but that's the fun of it! You're creating answers and solving problems, and that eventually turns into more pay and more freedom.

We have had opportunities to quit in everything we've done. I'm so glad we didn't. There were many times we felt defeated, and during one such time after moving to Ohio, we almost quit our business. Nothing seemed to be paying off. Broke, frustrated, and disgusted, at one point we prayed, "God, show us what to do and confirm we are on the right path." That very morning a package was delivered by FedEx to our front door, and in it was a teaching series called "Don't Quit." God knows where you are, and He has answers for your every need.

> You must believe in what you're doing—that you can do it and should do it—or you will lack motivation.

Sometimes we think we need more than we have to make it, but God always asks you to use what you have before He can give you anything else. What do you have to work with? What can you do with what you have? Success on any level, wherever you're at, is making the most out of what you have. That's how you measure personal success. Are you wasting what you already have? Are you passing over the opportunities in your life regularly? That's a poor mindset. You don't have to run a business to be an entrepreneur in everything you do. You can envision and grasp every opportunity around you.

I encourage you to wait ninety days if you think you need to make a major purchase in your business. It's better to have options than to have debt. If the need is recurring, it probably is a substantial need. There will be plenty of time to enjoy the fruit of your labor down the road, but starting out is not the time to spend.

Build a Team

Initially, you may need to outsource some of the needs your business has that family members can't supply, but eventually you will want to develop some of the key leadership areas of your family enterprise. In a year, who are the key players you will need to help you succeed?

It's important to have a trustworthy sounding board of people whom you can bounce ideas and strategies off of and get the best development of products, marketing, and distribution. As women, we process through communication. Talk out your answers to get clarity before you act. Don't act out of emotion or you may find yourself in trouble. Every business is built on wise counsel and sound planning. "Plans succeed through good counsel; don't go to war without wise advice" (Proverbs 20:18 NLT).

Your older children can be a great source of ideas for your business. When our children were teenagers, they helped us revamp our business and ministry methods and practices that were quickly becoming outdated. They still help us capture ideas on a new scale today. Gary and I can supply wisdom and past experience, but our children help us see the need to change and grow to stay relevant. We are slowly passing the baton of our knowledge, resources, and encouragement to them to take to a new level, wherever they go or in whatever they do in their future.

Another important role in the family business is the cheerleader. That was primarily my role, but to my joy, I see some of our children operating in this gift of encouragement as adults. I could see the potential in my husband and our business helping people fix their money thing. I served as the encourager, especially when circumstances appeared discouraging. There needs to be someone in your family who is there to cheer everyone along, celebrating victories loud and strong, and rallying everyone around the vision when defeats scream louder. If your idea or business is a good one, perseverance through the hardships that visit every business is crucial. The cheerleader will make sure no one quits short of victory!

The other area that must be addressed is administrative assistance. Creativity and vision need the support of organization, documentation, and compliance with legal and standard business practices. Much of this can be outsourced to payroll and legal companies, but family members can provide some assistance in tasks.

And then there are the implementers who make it happen! Planning must happen, but then you must act on your plan. As the CEO, you can't be the doer. Develop the prototype or system and then employ those who will implement it as quickly as possible. Otherwise you will become bogged down with micromanaging and labor, and there's no one thinking, deciding, and overseeing. If this isn't your strong suit, decide who has the ability to direct the corporation while you create. It's important to get each area covered with competent leadership. Some of this happens organically in the beginning of the business, since we tend to go after our passion, but as the business grows, it becomes more formal by necessity.

> This is the New Vintage family business, an apprenticeship in the home that prepares and develops natural God-given talent and passions in each child while instilling vision, character, and leadership training.

Who in your circle of family or friends may be a sounding board, a cheerleader, and administrative help initially and down the road? Can any of your older children start out doing these functions and grow into one of these positions depending on their gifts? What training is required? No preparation is wasted and in all labor there's profit, so even if your family member pursues other areas down the road, the lessons, exposure, and business learning will put them way ahead of the pack! That's how you pass the baton at a higher level to them!

In every sound business there must be operations, sales, marketing, accounting, and fulfillment—and a good measure of hope—to continue to grow your business.

I see great corporations and ministries that are operated by adult children who grew up in the mindset and opportunities that surfaced in their parents' vocation or calling. It doesn't mean that is where every one of them will end up, but it is a great pattern that in strong families can emerge into a win-win for everyone involved.

Your children learn a lot about people, business, leadership, and enterprises as they observe and contribute to your business. Our five adult children serve in various positions today: Tim is a Pastor/Director, Amy is a Worship/Creative Director, Kirsten is a Writer/Speaker, Tom is a Media Arts Director/Evangelist, and Polly is a Hair/Makeup Artist who also serves us and her husband, who is our Children's Director and one of our corporation representatives. They all learned and honed their skill set at home in the family business.

This is the New Vintage family business, an apprenticeship in the home that prepares and develops natural God-given talent and passions in each child while instilling vision, character, and leadership training. The intangible rewards have been priceless, but there have been great tangible rewards, too. As a family we've seen the world together, developed stronger bonds between us, and experienced the fruit of laboring collaboratively toward a common vision.

Ask Yourself:

What is my "reason" for my business?

What is my dream for my business and life?

What is my map or pathway to reach that dream? Create a plan to give yourself the number of contacts and appointments to make your goal, breaking it down into goals for five years, one year, each month, each week, and each workday.

What will you need to let go of to commit to that goal for the next 90 days?

How will you handle family needs? Or how will you incorporate them into the 90-day game plan?

What will be the shared reward if together you reach your goal in 90 days?

Building business and learning to do life as a team brings rewards!

What are you passionate about? What area could you start to develop and learn in?

....
....
....
....
....

What is your dream for your business and life? What step could you take in the next 90 days?

....
....
....
....
....

What will you need to let go of to commit to that goal for the next 90 days?

....
....
....
....
....

How will you handle family needs or incorporate them into your 90-day game plan?

....
....
....
....
....

The Vintage Challenge

Go on a picnic: My family has always enjoyed picnics, whether we did it in our backyard or went to the park. There's nothing more timeless than a picnic basket packed with delicious treats on a beautiful day. Spread a blanket out on the grass and watch the clouds roll by as you make memories with your family. It's great because it forces everyone to eat together and talk, but it's still fun for the kids. Just imagine all the fun you could have when you share a picnic with your loved ones!

Skip the shower—take a bath: Sometimes we get so busy helping everyone else that we neglect ourselves. When you find a spare moment from your busy schedule, why not dedicate a little time to you? I always loved when Gary came home from work and watched the kids for a little while so I could have some "me" time. It's not an everyday event, but it's definitely needed. A bubble bath is a great way to relax and splurge on some "me" time!

Write a handwritten letter and mail it: Handwritten letters are the ultimate vintage staple, and one I am personally sad to leave behind! It means a lot when you handwrite a letter to your spouse, mother, or friend. Or you could even get a pen pal! Why not go vintage and try it out?

Wash your dishes by hand: I usually prefer a dishwasher, but sometimes it's nice to get the accomplished feeling of washing the dishes by hand. It's also a great opportunity to sort through your thoughts or blow off some steam. If nothing else, it does make you appreciate some of the improvements we've made since the vintage era!

Take a TV and Social Media Sabbath: Take a day to rest from TV, movies, social media, and even the Internet! Try playing board games, cards, or kickball outside as a family instead.

Pick up a new hobby with your family: There's so much media entertainment for children, but they miss out on the fun of having *real* hobbies—the ones that involve doing things with other people, face-to-face, and developing skills. Not to mention that *you* miss out, too. Try out some new, fun hobbies and see what you're missing out on. Buy canvases and paint, play tennis, scrapbook, or play baseball with your family at your local baseball park. There's a whole world of fun for you and your family to explore!

Have dinner as a family: Whether you cook or get takeout, all of your family needs to sit down and enjoy a meal together at least a couple times a week. Our family was always very busy, but our meals together kept us connected. This means that your children don't take their food to their room or to somewhere else in the house, and this does *not* happen in front of your television. It's only a couple nights a week—the TV can wait, right?

Grow a garden (or let your kids): It can be therapeutic to garden a little every week. If you don't have a green thumb, though, why not encourage one of your kids to grow some flowers? Gary and I helped Kirsten plant mammoth sunflowers when she was little, and she loved running outside every day to water them. It was a great way to teach her responsibility and get her outside!

The "what" game: This was a fun game we used to play to get our kids out of the habit of saying "what." You know how it can be. We would say their name, and they'd respond with a sassy, *"What?"* So instead of saying "what," they needed to say, "Ma'am?" or "yes?" or something that sounded nicer. The game was that they had a potential dollar to earn if they didn't say "what" in a certain period of time (a week). If they did, they lost one of their quarters. The kids loved it. We would take them somewhere to spend their money on a toy when they had saved enough. It was a great way to reward our children for having a good attitude. You can make doing the right thing fun!

A fun way to have a fun day: Have each of your children write their perfect family fun day description, and then each week draw one the night before so you know what the next day involves. We had great fun doing this each week, and our activities covered everything from skiing to filming our own movie called *Ninja Nannies*, in which a family with disobedient children hired a ninja to come and straighten out their dysfunctional kids. When needed, the ninja would appear randomly from odd places. This was Tom's venture, and of course, he played the ninja, climbing in and out of our dryer for effect!

PART 3

Your Vintage Family

THE DYNAMICS THAT MAKE IT WORK

Our baby, Kirsten, graduating from kindergarten in our Faith Life Home Educators homeschool graduation program.

You're never too young to be excited about Christmas.

Drenda and Tim, 1987.

Peace of Mind

GETTING CHILDREN TO LISTEN

"A child who is allowed to be disrespectful to his parents will not have true respect for anyone."

BILLY GRAHAM

When my son Timothy was a small toddler, he was very mobile and always on the go. One day we were over at my in-laws' house and somehow Timothy escaped the house. It seemed as though he was with us one moment and gone the next. When we realized it, we frantically started searching. My husband ran out the door and toward the road. Sure enough, there was Timothy, toddling toward the traffic. My husband would not be able to reach him in time, so he yelled loudly, "Timothy, STOP! Come to Daddy!" Timothy instantly stopped in his tracks, turned and walked toward his daddy. Thank God he was an obedient child because we had disciplined him enough that he responded at our commands. It saved his life that day.

How many times have you seen a parent have the "On the count of three, you better obey or you're going to be in trouble" conversation with their child, only to hesitate at "two" when they see it's not working? How many times have you done it yourself?

I used to try this tactic to make my children obey, but it only works if you follow through on the count of three. If you don't enforce the consequences, you can count all day long. Think about it like this: if your child walked out into the street and you saw a car coming and told them to come back, would you want them to obey you immediately or on the count of three? Respect for authority can determine the outcome in a life-or-death situation, and I want my children to obey me in the second it counts.

In fact, my grown-up kids now joke that our "count of three" game was how many spankings they were going to get for continuously disobeying. So if Gary gave them instruction, and they whined and pitched a fit instead of obeying immediately, Gary would say, "That's two." You'll find that you get a lot better results with that tactic.

Discipline isn't a fun topic. It doesn't seem "spiritual" or important. It's also controversial right now, and you probably have a strong opinion about the way you do it—even if that way means no way at all. I understand. And because I understand, you can have the confidence that I don't want to waste your time on something that is not going to change your family life for the better. But this will. The information in this chapter has the power to make or break a family, and I've seen the evidence of that repeatedly.

You've invested this much time into seeing a change in your family, and I don't want to see you short-circuit yourself now. Stay determined and stay focused as you read what I'm about to share. Continue forward prayerfully and be sensitive to what God is speaking to you. This chapter is a game-changer, but it's up to you to make the play.

What Is the Right Balance?

I see so many Christians make the mistake of saying, "I trust God, so I can let my kids do what they want. God will watch out for them." Plain and simple, if you don't discipline children, you are abusing them in one way or another. On the other hand, I see parents who use discipline in place of love, which is another huge mistake. Discipline is so crucial in your children's life, but there's a right and wrong way to do it. Without love is the wrong way.

What is the right balance?

On one side of the equation are parents who beat and yell at their kids, which is abusive and creates rebellion and resentment or fear. The other side of the equation has parents who let their children walk over them. Their kids could commit murder and get off with a warning! You know how it goes: the moment the parent appears to be serious about bringing discipline, the child delivers an unconvincing performance of high-pitched whining, tears, and pleadings. The parent relents, hugs their precious one, whose tears instantly evaporate, and the child squirms out of their parent's arms and runs off to play.

My kids would observe this in other families and say, "That parent just got played." If you fall for that, you teach your child to manipulate you. You teach them that with enough drama, enough excuses, and enough games, they can get out of anything. Have you ever met any adults with that same attitude? They are not fun people to be around!

God gave us instruction to train our children up in the way they should go. I don't care how much you love God, or how much you pray, or how much you volunteer, or how much you trust God, if you don't raise your children with boundaries and consequences, you are sending them toward a hard fall.

When my son Tim was four years old, I got called out of

church service to come get him from his preschool class. When the teacher explained his disobedience in class, I said, "Okay," and walked Tim to the restroom and disciplined him. I brought him back to the class, and the teacher looked on in shock and said, "You're the only parent who's ever done that! Everyone else makes excuses for their child and doesn't care what I say."

If you have to be brought out of church service to deal with your child because they did something wrong, you need to enforce some consequences. If the teachers cringe when you check your child into children's church or daycare, you have a problem! Your child should not be a repeat offender in class.

You have to discipline and train children God's way. He told us how to do it. God wants good examples and good fruit, and He wants you to educate your children and raise them up. That's why you have to teach and train them. And in different phases of their life, there are different things they need to learn and different ways you need to teach them.

Don't Get Played

First, realize that we have all made parental mistakes, but we can't let our children use our mistakes to worm their way out of discipline. When we made a mistake, we went to our children and said, "Mom and Dad made a mistake, but we're still in authority. You still need to obey us. I lost my temper, something went wrong on my end, but that is not an excuse for you to act out." We didn't let them control us.

Children try almost anything to convince their parents why they shouldn't be disciplined, and why it was somebody else's fault, and then they don't receive any punishment. That trains children that if they can put on the tears, and if they can manipulate people, there won't be consequences for their actions.

We once knew a sweet couple that always believed the best in people. That was a great strength they had, but it became their downfall in parenting. When their children got in trouble, they immediately took their child's defense. They would ask their child, "Did you do that?" and when their child said no, that was the end of the discussion. Whether there were one or twenty witnesses, they couldn't believe their children would deceive them. These kids grew uncontrollable, fell away from God, and continued to manipulate and blame others for their problems. Meanwhile, their parents still took false responsibility for their actions.

Establish Your Authority

I believe it's better to be on the stricter side (with lots of love) than be too lenient (which usually is accompanied by lack of attention for the child). The reason I say that is because even in what some would call strict environments, at least the children are learning respect for authority. If they have respect for authority, they are teachable. However, a child that doesn't respect authority can't be mentored. They will lie and justify their way out of training.

The first thing you want to teach your child is to *respect your authority*. If your children don't respect your authority, they won't respect God's authority. You must show them that you care deeply for their well-being, and it is your God-given job to teach them right from wrong. They must understand you are in charge, and that you have a God mandate to bring them up under subjection to authority and the Word of God. You can't train a child who doesn't respect you. Respect is a result of being lovingly consistent and following through with what you say. Otherwise, you'll say the words, but they won't listen because you have never established your place of authority.

Discipline and structure are not wrong or abusive when carried out alongside love. When Gary or I had to discipline our children, we always first explained why. We would say, "I must discipline you because you chose to disobey what I said." Afterward, we gave them a hug and told them how much we loved them and didn't want bad choices to bring them bad consequences in their life. That put discipline in perspective for them. Then they understood that we had to discipline them *because* we loved them too much to let them disobey. Remember the agape form of love and communication discussed in chapter six? It applies here, too.

> The first thing you want to teach your child is to respect your authority. If your children don't respect your authority, they won't respect God's authority.

I hear parents telling me often, "My kids fight all day long and it's driving me crazy!" Inevitably an argument will erupt between siblings, but it must be dealt with or it will create an environment of chaos in your home. Whenever our kids got into disagreements with one another, we talked it out with them, and it always ended with them giving one another hugs and telling their sibling, "I love you." Sometimes it required one (or both) saying, "I'm sorry," and the other saying, "I forgive you," training them early on to apologize and forgive. This was also a lesson in humility, and to avoid being thus humbled, my children rarely got into heated arguments. Sure, they would pester one another, but we did not tolerate yelling or strife—ever. You must remember that you are creating a culture in your home by what you tolerate and what you demonstrate. Remind your children how much you love them and how much they need to love one another.

I get calls from moms in tears saying, "My two-year-old is

driving me nuts. I can't do this anymore." If you're an adult, how is it possible that a two-year-old is driving you nuts? I say to that mom, "You're in authority, remember? The two-year-old is under your authority, and you're not exercising your authority if the two-year-old is running the house." Do yourself a favor: love them enough to discipline them early, so you don't end up with a fifteen-year-old acting like they are still two.

Whether it's the early years, the middle years, or the teen years of your child's life, the most important thing you can do is to establish and reestablish that you are in authority. If you don't, your children won't understand God's authority and will rebel against God. They will disrespect the things of God. They will think it's okay to treat other authorities the same way they treat you.

Parents come to me and say, "My children were in church every Sunday. Why did they rebel?" *Because of authority.* They didn't learn how to respect authority at home, so now they don't respect God's authority or the authority of others. That's a dangerous place to be.

Staying Consistent

Consistency is probably the most important aspect behind discipline and boundary setting, because it ties love and discipline together. Without consistency, it is difficult for a child to understand the message you're trying to convey, which only frustrates them. People thrive under some structure; but when that structure varies and they don't know if a rule exists from one time to the next, they begin to feel resentful and distrusting. It's the same way with your children.

If a mom says yes to something, and the dad says no, that creates inconsistency. If you allow something one day and don't allow it another, that creates inconsistency. When there isn't consistency in discipline, children feel that you're disciplining them out of spite or personal anger.

With our children, we had a rule that they were not allowed to go to Gary and ask about something that I had already answered for them. They couldn't play us against each other and manipulate us to get the answer they wanted. I understand that in blended or divorced families this can get complicated, but although you can't control what your spouse does, *you* can choose to stay consistent.

We never let our children tear each other down and call each other names. My children also weren't allowed to dishonor Gary and me. The children knew that if they dishonored me, they would be in bad shape with Gary. There is an authority in the house, and there is a unity in the house that the children can rely on. A child might resent authority after having those consequences enforced, but in the long run a child values the sense of security that authority brings to a home. They know they are going to be fiercely protected and cared for. They know that you are going to keep your word.

> Without a vision for your children, they will perish. You have to keep the end result in mind so you know the steps to get you there. When you have the vision in front of you, you can make the hard decisions.

Deuteronomy 4:9 says, "Only be careful, and watch yourselves closely so that you do not forget the things your eyes have seen or let them fade from your heart as long as you live." Don't let God's Word fade from your heart. Teach it to your children. That's your goal. If you put the vision before you, it will be a whole lot easier to make the tough decisions. Anything that doesn't line up with your goal has to go.

"Where there is no vision, the people perish: but he that keepeth the law, happy is he" (Proverbs 29:18 KJV). Without a vision for your children, they will perish. You have to keep the end result in mind so you know the steps to get you there. When you have the vision in front of you, you can make the hard decisions.

Expectations and Consequences

First, lay out what is expected of your child. Have clear rules in place, and if you don't already have those rules, you can establish them by giving warnings. When your child is pitching a tantrum, if you haven't already drawn a line there, you need to establish your expectations.

Here is an example of how you might effectively communicate your expectation (training) and consequence (discipline): "We do not throw tantrums to get our way. I am in authority, and you need to obey my decision without a bad attitude. If you can't do that, I will discipline you, because I love you too much to let you act like that. God wants us to have quick and cheerful obedience." There's a clear *expectation* established, and a clear *consequence* if they don't meet that expectation. Now, because you've established that expectation, your child knows the consequence the next time they disobey. Of course, you have to follow through with that. Keep your word. Remind them of the expectation and consequence, and follow through when they disobey. It doesn't take many times before your children understand the expectation, and you won't have to constantly discipline. They will start to self-correct.

We rarely had to discipline our kids. They reached the age where they were testing our will, and once they saw that we were serious about our warnings, they were fine. And that respect for authority carried into their older years. We had to discipline them some as they grew into new stages and wanted to make sure the authority was still the rule, but it was rare.

The expectations you set for a three-year-old versus a ten-year-old are different. A three-year-old has an attention span of three minutes, so you have different expectations of them. The principles are the same, but the standard you would hold them to is less strict than for your ten-year-old. You wouldn't expect your three-year-old to take out the trash every day, but you could expect that of your ten-year-old. At the same time, you would expect your three-year-old to clean up their toys with your guidance.

The children's ministry for our church is a great example of these different levels of expectations. We have the same rules for the three-year-olds as we have for ten-year-olds, but they have different standards. In the three-year-old class, we aren't going to sit children down and make them listen to a teacher talk for forty-five minutes. We want to give them the same message and teach them the same principles as a normal church service, but we're going to do that on a platform that they understand. Instead of forty-five minutes, we're going to do it in five. We still expect them to listen to their teachers and obey, but we aren't going to set them up for failure, because we know that their attention spans are only a few minutes. So after they are taught their lesson, they get to go play and have a snack. If we deliver the same principles to the kids, but we give it to them on their level, they can receive that.

For the six- to ten-year-olds, we will deliver those principles on a different level. We will also hold them to a different standard. Instead of sitting five minutes for a lesson, we will do thirty minutes of teaching, videos, and skits to help them get the principles on their level.

The principles are always the same, but you may communicate that more simply for younger ages and your standards should reflect the age of the child. You don't have a long discussion about their mistake when a child is young. You need to make your message clear. You need to get four things across when you discipline your child: your expectation, the consequence, God's love, and your love.

If your child has an accident, you don't discipline them for that. You don't discipline a child for flipping over their milk. However, you do discipline a child if you told them to stop cutting up at the table, they disobeyed you, and then they flip over their milk.

In real life, a bad choice equals a bad consequence, so you need to establish consequences for them as you train them. You establish a rule, and if they disobey it, you discipline them. You don't wait until the point where you're angry. If you're angry, you waited too long to enforce the consequence. You should not be screaming or shouting at your child when you discipline them. When you do that, you do more damage to their self-esteem by berating them with your words, threatening them, and telling them how mad you are. People who don't establish expectations and enforce consequences end up acting out in anger toward their child verbally or physically, and that is far worse than disciplining them calmly and consistently in love.

Some parents worry, "Well, if we discipline them, they might rebel against God." I say, if you don't establish expectations and consequences for them, they *are* going to rebel against God! I take a strong stance on this, because it's crucial to the success of your family. The Bible makes it clear that if you don't discipline your children, you are standing by as they make their way to destruction. There is no gray area in the Bible on discipline, yet many Christians are silent on the matter. I think that is one of the biggest causes of the dysfunction we see in families and classrooms today.

Everyone needs discipline, because it trains us not to make the same mistakes repeatedly. It's like the saying, "Give a man a fish, and you feed him for a day; show him how to catch fish, and you feed him for a lifetime." God wants to give you the discipline to maintain the good things He gives you.

Why do you think you're dealing with some of the issues in your life? Was it caused by lack of self discipline? Perhaps God is letting you walk through paying off your debt instead of getting a miraculous deliverance, because He wants you to understand the discipline it takes to stay out of debt. Perhaps He wants you to work through your marriage issues because you have a character flaw that needs to be dealt with. He's not just going to wave a wand and make every problem go away. Character that comes from discipline is more valuable than the quick solution.

> In real life, a bad choice equals a bad consequence, so you need to establish consequences for them as you train them. You establish a rule, and if they disobey it, you discipline them.

We want everything quick and easy, but God wants to make the change last in your life. There are people who win the lottery, and it ruins their life. Why? They don't have the discipline or the character developed for that kind of money, so they don't know how to maintain it.

When we were in New York City at Battery Park that overlooks the Statue of Liberty and Ellis Island, I noticed how clean Battery Park was in contrast to around the city where trash is common. Even with all of the tourists pouring in, it looked as though somebody had been maintaining it. We happened to ask the owner of a restaurant by the harbor, and he smiled and said, "A lot of homeless men come by the restaurant every night and ask for our leftover food. We have to throw it away, so I could just give it to them, but I want to help them move past living off of handouts. I tell them that if they pick up the trash in Battery Park, I will pay them with the food."

That business owner was teaching them the discipline it would require to get a job and get off the streets. Instead of giving those homeless men something that would fix their problem for a moment, he decided to invest something in them—a principle in them—that could change their situation forever.

And that is what you are doing for your children. Instead of giving them quick fixes to satisfy their problems for a moment, invest principles in them that will guide them for a lifetime. Give them the decision-making ability to solve problems for themselves.

Visiting Lady Liberty near Battery Park with Tim, Kirsten, Gary, Amy, and our son-in-love Jason.

Is the level of discipline you have established in your family a healthy balance of love alongside expectations and consequences? How can you improve it?

....

....

....

....

What is your greatest struggle in discipline? How can you overcome it? (Read Hebrews 12:11.)

....

....

....

....

....

Do you enforce consequences consistently? Or do you pick and choose your battles?

....

....

....

....

....

What can you take away from this chapter and apply to your everyday life?

....

....

....

....

....

....

Tim's
⋙ MONOGRAPH ⋘
MY SECOND BORN

amily is a word representing more than a group of people that can sometimes look like a part of a circus act—it is God's design. There are times where it really seems to represent a circus act, though. You will have to remind yourself of God's design throughout the adventure, especially if you're one of five children or a parent! My name is Tim. I'm the number two kid/rug rat/man-child/Keesee. There were five kids and two adults in the Keesee family circus. Our little circus acts have taken us across the world and filled every dull moment with laughing, meaning, and learning. Sometimes our little circus was full of tears, but one thing was for sure, it was always a circus worth seeing! Even with seven in my family, it never seemed crowded, and I can't imagine my life without any one of my family members. They all taught me so much about life, and the lessons were taught in what could appear to be a five-ring circus.

Amy was the oldest and wisest. We all looked to her example growing up. She was as steady and loving as the very best and closest of friends. Mother's words of wisdom were always echoed in her, and she taught me to be kind and tender. Once, when I was about eight, I had the bright idea to reenact something I'd seen in a movie. Amy was going to be the victim of my cruelty. In the movie, a guy faked a heart attack to get the jump on his unsuspecting captor ($20 to the sibling who can guess the movie). A perfect opportunity presented itself for me to try my new trick. Amy and I were walking into the house after jumping on our trampoline.

"Oh, I'm having a heart attack!" I cried, dropping to my knees and grasping my chest. I'm not sure why this seemed like a good idea, but to an eight-year-old, it was a chance to put all of my acting skills to the test. It worked. Amy stopped, and with panic in her eyes she ran to me. As I rolled onto my back, she leaned over me, calling out my name. When I opened my eyes, I was shocked. Tears were running down her face. "Oh, gosh, I was just joking." I got in trouble for that one, but I'll always remember the concern on her face. Amy has always looked to the needs of others more than her own. In fact, Amy and I have never even had a real argument in all our years growing up together. This was the first ring of our circus.

My brother, Tom, born three years after me, helped teach me to dream big, to be competitive, to know what was cool and to fly. The lesson in flight came one beautiful summer evening. Tom and I were "taking turns" riding the family horse. With a big family, sometimes you have to share. There was plenty of room to ride on our farm, but we only had one horse. This resulted in a lot of waiting and the constant asking of, "When is it my turn?" Well, I had waited and waited, but Tom was taking his good old time. I waved, yelling from a distance, but still, he rode on.

Finally, in desperation, I went to tell my parents of the horrible injustice concerning the horse. It didn't take long before my mother came out and ordered the change in turns. At last, this was my chance to feel the wind in my hair and to ride like a cowboy into the sunset. Our horse, Holly, was a bit lazy and round. She wasn't one to give up the reins easily to her riders just as my brother Tom wasn't planning to give the reins over to me without a fight.

I reached the opening in the trail where the path became straight, which was my chance to get some speed. "Yeehaa, get going!" I yelled. The horse broke into a gallop down the trail. Little did I know Tom had planned revenge.

There was an unspoken rule among us siblings: you don't bring the parents in to settle the score unless it's absolutely the last resort. I had broken this rule when I brought in reinforcements to guarantee my fair ride time. Tom hid in the bushes, and as I neared, he leaped out. All at once, I had a floating sensation as I was being catapulted. I was flying! Horses can stop on a dime, but their riders seldom do. I was in the air, flying right over the horse's head, but I soon realized I wasn't flying—I was falling! *Thud* . . .

I think Tom was as surprised as the horse and I were when he saw me launch. I lived, and for a brief moment I got to feel what it would be like to be a bird. In spite of moments like those, we always would work things out and ten minutes later be laughing and playing, moving on to the next big adventure. We shared a room for years. When we built a bigger house, we had separate rooms, but we still shared. We didn't want to be apart. Tom has taught me a lot about perspective, adventure, and forgiveness. He always brought a great deal of excitement into my life as the third ring of our family circus.

Polly is the fourth-born Keesee. She values understanding and planning. We are and have often been a fly-by-the-seat-of-our-pants family, from skydiving and bungee jumping to traveling across the world. Polly would keep us in order and has taught me that planning is a good thing. She is fun, sweet, and beautiful. I'm so thankful for her.

Once, our family was traveling across Europe together. Seven people make this type of travel very interesting. Planes, trains, automobiles, and boats can be exhausting, but even more difficult is not losing anybody. We often had to split up into two taxis with drivers who didn't speak English and hope everyone would make it to the same place.

We traveled by train and subway extensively. The subways stop for about thirty seconds, just long enough for people to jump off and the new wave to jump on at the same time, creating a clash of chaos. In one event in the underground Metro in Paris, the packed train pulled up, and we tried to jump in there like the locals. The train car was too full, but in the chaotic rush Polly and Kirsten (ages eleven and eight) somehow got onboard without our seeing them, the doors closed, and they were trapped. The rest of us spotted an opening several train cars down and ran for it, climbing in quickly. It all happened so fast. My two little sisters didn't know we were a few train cars down, and our car was so crowded we couldn't tell where everyone was.

Several stops of people getting on and off went by, and we approached our exit and Dad yelled, "This is us, kids!" The train stopped, and we grabbed our belongings and jumped off. My family gathered on the platform to regroup and do a head count. "Everyone here?" Mom asked. "Wait, where are Polly and Kirsten? Who has them? They got on with us, right?"

The Metro station was swarming with people. As the crowd cleared, there was Polly and Kirsten standing down the line a ways, looking panicked and searching the crowd for us. They had been paying attention to Mom when she showed them how to navigate the Metro, and they remembered which stop to get off at. We may have never found them again if they would have gotten off too soon or ridden the train too far. Maybe that's why Polly loves attention to detail so much today! Performing in the fourth ring of our circus was Polly.

Kirsten is the fifth-born Keesee. Kirsten's middle name is Joy, and she brings my whole family a great deal of joy. She has a big heart and is a smart girl. She started college work at the age of fifteen and graduated at a very young age, and hopefully she will read this and catch my typos. Kirsten has taught me to be a protector. There's twelve years between us. She was always my little buddy. I would read her books and watch Aristocats over and over with her.

> You don't hope for good kids; you make them. There were so many times people would say to my parents, "I wish our kids were as well behaved as yours." This is your job as a parent. Make them that way.

There are a lot of stories from Kirsten, but a simple moment I will always remember occurred while traveling. There were many times in our travels where we would only have one hotel room available to us. This would result in pallet parties and kids covering the floor. It was late one night, and we were all exhausted from the day's escapades. The lights were turned out, and we were all supposed to go to sleep, but someone had to go to the bathroom, a dangerous walk to get to the door with people everywhere.

"Ouch!" Kirsten yelled out.

"Oh, I'm sorry," said the bathroom traveler. "Are you okay?"

"I'm okay," Kirsten replied, and the bathroom traveler went on their way, arms stretched out to find the door in the dark.

I could tell by the sound of Kirsten's little seven-year-old voice that she was crying. I crawled over to her and put my arm around her and whispered, "Sorry you got stepped on." Her little tears were so sweet. She didn't want whoever it was who stepped on her to feel bad even though it hurt. Just being there to comfort her meant a lot to me. She was the fifth ring of our five-ring circus.

Finally, we get to the ringmasters, my parents. It was their job to orchestrate all five acts of our five-ring circus. They had to coach us through some performances that were poorly put together. Some of the acts were funny; some were serious. Some of the acts were discontinued, and others encouraged. A parent's jobs are many. It's sad to see so many parents opting out of their roles as the leaders and educators of their children, as the directors of their families. It isn't the school's job to teach and mentor children; it is the parents. What are the kids learning? And, even more important, what lessons are they being taught outside of the classroom by their peers? Hanging out with friends, they will learn a lot, maybe just as much as what they will learn at the desk. They will learn a myriad of things no child should be exposed to. Parents must jump in there and be the guardians of their children.

We aren't truly a free nation without parents being involved in what lessons are learned. Let me explain. The future of our nation is in the minds of its youth. But who chooses the lessons the young will learn? Do those people have a desire to see God's truth spread? What is their agenda? In twenty years, we will all see their agenda unfold as the next generation begins to vote and carry the banner of their education. We are only one generation from any liberal restructuring of our nation. This is why parents must fulfill their God-given duties to train their children.

You don't hope for good kids; you make them. There were so many times people would say to my parents, "I wish our kids were as well behaved as yours." This is your job as a parent. Make them that way. They are clay to be molded, and each one will have natural tendencies, strengths, and weaknesses. But shape their futures. It isn't a weird controlling thing, but coaching, mentoring, and training. Most important, it's a loving thing. Demonstrate to them how to live.

My parents were full of love for each other and us kids. They demonstrated that your marriage comes first. It is vital to keep this even before your kids' needs. In fact, this is your child's greatest need. A healthy, happy marriage is an example of how to live in peace and will create security in the home. If the ringmasters don't know what is going on and which acts to keep in the show, it will be chaos. The ringmasters are in charge.

My parents were a unified unit, and they knew the behaviors they wanted to see in our lives. We didn't have arguments with our parents as kids; we knew better. If we messed with Mom or were disrespectful, we all knew it was only a matter of time before Dad came home. Live in peace. Have the difficult conversations and teach your kids how to act and live.

Growing up, I was in the second ring of the circus, giving my siblings plenty of stories about me. I'm now married with kids of my own. My wife and I started our own circus. We're now the ringmasters and responsible for keeping everything headed in the right direction. It's fun and a new adventure, but I'm not completely unprepared. I've observed my parents. I remember the adventures we had together, the life lessons learned, and the examples that went before us.

Each person is different and has their unique quirks and strengths. Each person is in their own ring. It isn't a competition. You will have to discover the uniqueness of your own children just as I am doing with my own. All my siblings were very different from one another and brought different strengths to the ring. Celebrate those differences. It isn't about being perfect, but learning through the moments that truly do belong in the circus. While I'm writing this, my one-year-old daughter is riding me like a horse and rubbing a Nutra-Grain bar in my hair, and I wouldn't trade it for the world. It really is like a circus—a wonderful, meaningful adventure called the family circus.

Getting some sibling perspective on life!

Make an Impression

THE EVIDENCE YOUR CHILDREN NEED

> "Each of us will have our own different ways of expressing love and care for the family. But unless that is a high priority, we may find that we may gain the whole world and lose our own children."
>
> MICHAEL GREEN

Faith is much more than religion. Faith is the evidence or result of what you've believed in your life—whether that was faith in God, in debt, in fear, or in failure. Since faith is the evidence of things hoped for, the evidence in your life points to where your faith is. Your faith produces your outcome. Your children need to see the goodness of God growing up. Your children also need your *example,* because it is the example you set for your children that tells of the goodness of God. When you combine the two, you have a powerful combination: *faith by example.* What you model for your children, they will act out. What you put before your children, and the principles you instill into your children, will be mirrored in their own lives.

Timothy was a young pastor in Ephesus. It was rare for somebody his age to have that level of responsibility in the church. Persecution began to break out against the church, and Paul wrote Timothy a letter of encouragement. "I am reminded of your sincere faith, *which first lived in your grandmother Lois and in your mother Eunice and, I am persuaded, now lives in you also.* For this reason I remind you to fan and to flame the gift of God . . . For the Spirit God gave us does not make us timid, but gives us power, love, and self-discipline" (2 Timothy 1:5–7).

What Paul is telling Timothy is so profound. "Timothy, don't let fear overcome you in this time of persecution. Remember what you learned at *home*." Paul goes on to say, "But as for you [Timothy], continue in what you have learned and *become convinced of, because you know those from whom you learned it, and how from infancy you've known the Holy Scriptures,* which are able to make you wise for salvation through faith in Jesus Christ" (2 Timothy 3:14–15).

So where is a child supposed to see the Kingdom of God? At home!

Timothy had become convinced of the foundations he learned at home, and because he had learned responsibility and how to handle authority, he was promoted. So few young men are taught to handle responsibility today. Most men are scared spitless (as Gary says) of responsibility. They've not been mentored by fathers and have not learned how to handle responsibility or authority, and so life is a big scary place to them. That is why the training ground of the family is an amazing system to raise up leaders.

When we were desperately in debt, our kids saw that. They knew they couldn't get happy meals or new clothes. They saw our cars smoke when we started them. They knew the old farmhouse was cold in the wintertime and that Daddy had to run down to the gas station to get $2 of diesel fuel to run the fuel furnace to heat the house at night. So when we discovered how the Kingdom of God operates, we made sure that we brought our children along on that journey as well.

We began to have family prayer. We began to write down what we needed. We put it before the Lord, and together we would check off those things. I didn't want my kids' perspective of God to be an old cold farmhouse or rundown cars. I wanted their perspective of God to be more than enough, needs met, protection, and answers. I wanted my children to know that God meets all of our needs.

Today, my greatest thrill in life is my family. They are all serving God. They're blessed and prospering, and they're in the ministry (both marketplace ministry and church ministry) because they want to and not because we ever made them. We always had to tell our children, "Okay, it's time to leave church now. We have to go home." We were the ones who had to pull them back! Listen, your kids need to see demonstration of the Kingdom of God at home, in your life.

> Husbands and wives should say, "Kids, follow us as we follow Christ," and the evidence should be there for them to see the Kingdom of God. Otherwise, without the evidence of God's goodness and the personal relationship with Him, religion is rules and regulations.

Why is there an old perception that the pastor's kids are some of the wildest kids around the church? Because their dad preaches that God can do all things at church, but there's no evidence at home to back up what they hear. They know how dad treats mom, and vice versa. They know if God really came through at home. And because a lot of people don't experience the reality of the Kingdom, they leave. That's not God's fault. The reality of the Kingdom is always there—you just have to bring it into your circumstances.

If your kids see something good, your kids will want it. Don't they talk about being someone great? Don't they talk about the heroes in their life? Paul said follow me as I follow Christ. Husbands and wives should say, "Kids, follow us as we follow Christ," and the evidence should be there for them to see the Kingdom of God. Otherwise, without the evidence of God's goodness and the personal relationship with Him, religion is rules and regulations.

What Model Are You Setting?

My daughter Kirsten was working in the three-year-old class at children's church with another teacher, and she had one child who was unmanageable. He would get angry and fall on the floor screaming. They had to call his parents back.

When the parents came to remove him from the class, he ran away from his parents and screamed, "No! No!" until his father offered him candy. In the lull, the other teacher expressed why they had to call them back, and the parents listened silently. When she finished, the dad said, "He's tired." He looked at his son who was gloating in his arms with a smile and a piece of candy. "Are you tired, honey?" The little boy shook his head. The dad listed more excuses. Meanwhile, the little boy had squirmed out of his arms and was throwing and destroying more things in the classroom.

Kirsten stood there in awe. Here they had come to the parents with real concerns, and the parents didn't respect their authority or even care what they said.

The mom, who hadn't said a word, timidly spoke up. "Well, he is acting very disobedient and—"

Explosive yelling from her husband cut her off. He pointed a finger in his wife's face, told her not to talk about her son that way, backed her into a corner, and continued to yell at her. The mother didn't act as though it was an unusual occurrence.

That child didn't respect his teacher's authority because his dad didn't respect authority. And that little boy had an anger issue and disrespect for women, because that is what he saw modeled by his father. He was only acting out what was modeled for him.

Children reflect their home life. They are an honest mirror of their parents in many ways. You can put on a good face at church, but your children expose the life you live at home. They'll say their parents have been fighting, or their mom's boyfriend isn't very nice, or their dad has a special drink that makes him mean. Children are an honest reflection of you!

Gary is a deer hunter, and through hunting God taught him how the Kingdom operates and how faith can help us receive what we need. Gary doesn't hunt deer; he "receives" them every season. When Tim was nine years old, he came to Gary two days before deer season and asked Gary to take him hunting. When Gary asked him why he thought he'd get a deer, Tim said, "Oh, that's easy. I'll do it like you do, Dad. I'll do it by faith."

Gary wasn't sure about taking him out, so Tim bargained that if he could hit a milk jug from ten yards, Gary would take him out. Tim was so small that when he held up the gun, it was nearly bigger than he was! He shot all around the milk jug and missed it by yards. Gary told Tim he couldn't go.

That night Tim ran up to Gary and tugged on his shirt. "I have an idea, Dad," he said. "I want to try shooting the gun on my other shoulder. I think I can aim it that way." This time, at ten yards, he hit it. Gary agreed to take him out that Monday morning, but Tim was only allowed to shoot a deer if it came within ten yards.

Sunday morning before church, Tim came out of his room with a dollar bill in his hand. He told Gary, "Dad, I have to sow my seed at church, and then I'm going to get my deer just like you do." My heart melted. It was a proud moment to watch my little boy copy what he had seen his father do many times before, honoring God with his faith and finances. We agreed with him and sowed his seed in the offering. Gary spent that night show-ing Tim pictures of deer and where to shoot them.

Gary and Tim went out hunting Monday morning. Gary was nervous. Here was our nine-year-old who had seen the Kingdom work in our lives, and we wanted him to have the same expe-rience. Gary wanted Tim to get a deer more than he wanted one for himself, because Tim's understanding of the laws of the Kingdom were being formed right there.

> Faith Works Every Time.

Gary helped Tim get in the tree stand. Gary stood on the platform and had Tim sit right between his legs. Gary told Tim he'd tap him with his foot if there was a shot Tim could take; otherwise he wasn't supposed to shoot.

Forty-five minutes went by. Gary didn't see anything, but suddenly there was the sound of a stick snapping. Gary looked down, and right below them was a seven-point buck standing at the base of their tree . . . ten yards from Tim!

Gary tapped Tim, who raised his gun as the deer began to walk out, but Tim didn't shoot. Gary thought Tim was too ner-vous, but then he realized that Tim was struggling to get the safety off. The deer wandered another ten yards farther. Gary heard a click, the gun fired, and the deer dropped instantly. Tim and Gary came running into the house shouting and cheering. Tim got his picture with his deer in the local sports magazine, and he was thrilled. Because that was Tim's first deer, and he received it by faith, we paid to have the head mounted and hung it on his bedroom wall.

Tim got a wood burning set that Christmas, and one day

Gary noticed Tim making something. He asked Tim to see it. Tim was finishing the last letter on a plaque he was going to hang right under his deer head. It said: *Faith Works Every Time.*

For the rest of his life, Tim has that deer mount to remind him of how good God is. He has that remembrance of the law of the Kingdom of God, and he has experience that faith really works every time. He had evidence of God's power instilled in him at a young age. Every child needs to have memories and reinforcements of the Kingdom of God. Without it, they're adrift. Your word is no better than someone else's. They need to see evidence!

What you model for your children, they will act out. What Gary modeled in front of Tim as a young boy he mirrored. If you smoke or drink alcohol in front of your children, your children will probably do the same, which is a dangerous game. Maybe you practice self-control with alcohol, but what if they develop an alcohol addiction? You have to be wise—Satan is looking for any place he can get a hold in the lives of your children. What example are you setting?

Show the Evidence of God in Your Life

When we built our dream house, we were moving out of a decrepit old farmhouse. The church wasn't paying us a salary at the time (per our request), but our board voted that when we moved into the new house they wanted to start paying us. We gathered the family around and told them, "The church has decided to pay us a small salary. We're going to use the money to build a swimming pool so that you know that God is good. Now every time you jump in that swimming pool, we want you to remember that God brought that pool. He paid for it because we're serving the Lord Jesus Christ, and I want you to know that God is good and wants to give you good things. Just always give Him your heart." Our children have enjoyed that swimming pool ever since. I want my children to experience what an awesome God we serve!

When I was homeschooling our children, and we hardly had two nickels to rub together, I always said, "I am going to take you kids to Europe." I had gone to Europe during high school, and I wanted to show it to my children. I pulled out pictures of Italy and France and showed them to them. I told them, "Some day I am going to take you there. By faith, we are going to do this."

By God's grace, several years later, we had the cash to pay for the trip. As a school project, I assigned each of the children a place we were going to visit. They had to map out where we were going and write papers on the places they wanted to see the most. I can still remember our seven-year-old Kirsten navigating the streets of France with her little roller backpack. I can see all of my family, in a single row, pulling their bags down the cobble streets. We spent three weeks traveling all over Europe.

My point is your children need to see the evidence of God's goodness in your life. Gary and I can tell story after story of God's goodness, and our children were a part of that. They saw the evidence. They saw faith by example. When I asked Kirsten when she was younger why she served God, she told me, "Growing up, it worked all the time. We lived by God's Word. We always prayed, we always saw God come through, and that's how I grew up. I never expected anything else."

"Start children off on the way they should go, and even when they are old they will not turn from it" (Proverbs 22:6).

Mentorship is crucial. When pressure comes, people revert to doing things the way they were trained. It's the habits and patterns you've established in your life. Your children will inherit your faith or your fears. Which one will it be?

Aristotle said, "We are what we repeatedly do. Excellence, then, is not an act, but a habit."

God is good. Once you experience the goodness of His Kingdom, why would you want to go someplace else? If we can train our children up and demonstrate that to our kids, we have succeeded. Parents, you're the key to demonstrating God's goodness!

Luke 6:40 says, "The student is not above the teacher, but everyone who is fully trained will be like their teacher." It's easier to hope they'll be above the teacher, not *like* their teacher. That can be a scary thought! Many children who grew up with alcoholic parents swear they will never drink alcohol, but years down the road they end up in the same place their parents were. Why is that? Because when pressure comes against us, we fall back on the way we were trained to live life. We may become the very thing we despised. We become like our teacher.

> Your children need to see the evidence of God's goodness in your life.

Fortunately, God sets us free from that cycle of dysfunction, and we can tap into His good and perfect system instead. We don't have to make the same mistakes our parents did. However, that cycle can work in your benefit if you are trained on the right system and mentored with the right example. If your children are taught to rely on God when difficult circumstances come, that is going to benefit their life.

Do you feel that you are living a life that exemplifies God's goodness to your children?

....

....

....

....

....

Does your family regularly have prayer time together? If not, where can you schedule it in?

....

....

....

....

....

Are there any areas in your life that you feel are representing God negatively to your children? What are those? How can you make a change there?

....

....

....

....

....

What can you take away from this chapter and apply to your everyday life?

....

....

....

....

....

Polly's MONOGRAPH

MY FOURTH BORN

My name is Polly Patton, and I am the fourth child in the Keesee family. I am twenty-three years old and have been married to my childhood crush for five years. Jon and I have one child, Ivory Anne, who is two years old. Yes, you heard me right; I've already been married for five years. Growing up in my family, I always saw marriage as positive and something that was of great value. I had a burning desire from a very young age to get married young and be a mom. There was only a couple of other things that I aspired to do some day, and that was be a hairstylist, use a cash register, wear fake nails, and be a professional ballerina in my spare time (kidding, kind of).

People ask, "What was it like growing up in the Keesee home? Is your family perfect?" to which I chuckle and say no! I don't believe any family is perfect or has it all together at any given moment, nor do we pretend to. We were just your average family who had amazing parents who always said yes to God no matter the circumstances. Since I wasn't the first or last child or the first girl in the family, I had to make my mark, and I did that by being the blunt, say whatever is on my mind, crazy child. I've been told I am the family comedian, but I'm not letting it go to my head. In my short life, I've seen God do a ton in my family and in Jon's and my life.

I can honestly say my childhood was amazing. It wasn't average; it was great. I was homeschooled, and with the church being new, we poured a ton of our time and effort as a family into it. Dancing was "me" time away from all the craziness of a big fun family. I was passionate about ballet and still am. Countless times I would be stranded at ballet waiting for my ride to arrive, and then I'd see my mom pull in the parking lot with a panicked face. My mom wasn't the normal soccer mom driving kids to every practice and reading a book in the car while she waited. With businesses, a church, and five kids, it just didn't happen like that. Yet with all the demands ministry and being an entrepreneur brings, my parents made us kids a priority. Nothing came before the health of our family, and I fully believe this is why all five kids still serve in the church and love God to this day, beating PK ("pastor's kid") statistics.

I will never forget being twelve years old when my dad called a family meeting. He began to cry and explain that he didn't think he could pastor anymore, because he saw the strain on the family. To this day I can see my dad's face, and it still makes me tear up. My parents have always been transparent and honest with us. In that moment, I realized nothing is as valuable to my dad as me and my siblings; and though the church and his businesses can be my competitor for his time, he would drop them in a second for our family's sake. From that moment on I wanted to serve my parents and the church in any way I could. I saw the great pressure and stress being in ministry brings.

My mom always made life fun, even when we didn't have any money. I cried the day we left the old farmhouse and wanted to stay. I didn't have to carry the stress the 1800s farmhouse brought to my parents. To me it was a wonderful place where I had so many great memories. Be wise not to talk about money issues or stressful life problems in front of your children, because they will carry that stress and lose their childlike thinking and imagination.

> My parents modeled for us that God is real. We don't just talk about Him and pray to Him, but we see the evidence in our life. I've seen too much to ever question if God is real.

The time before cell phones and before the world became so electronic-driven was a great, simple time, and I often dream of returning to it. As kids, we would play outside all day, making mud pies, riding bikes, building tree houses, and running through the neighbor's corn fields (oops, maybe my mom doesn't know about that yet). Nowadays, kids don't know how to play anymore. You send them outside, and they're back at the door whining for their PlayStation five minutes later. Jon and I have vowed to raise our kids in an atmosphere where they can create and imagine.

The life that I "played" when I was little is now the life I'm living. I will soon be a graduate of cosmetology school. I married the man I've loved since I was little. I have a beautiful daughter. We've just purchased our dream home . . . and I even have fake nails. Ha-ha! God has blessed all my siblings and me tremendously, and the awesome news is God is no respecter of persons. My dad always said, "If you take care of God's people, He will take care of you." Growing up in ministry, we did give things up—Sunday lunches were spent counseling other families, late nights were spent at the church cleaning, and we didn't always have our parents' 24/7 attention—but we were raised to serve people, and in doing that God will make sure every desire is fulfilled.

My parents modeled for us that God is real. We don't just talk about Him and pray to Him, but we see the evidence in our life. I've seen too much to ever question if God is real. Your children need to have this picture before they are on their own in order to survive in a very corrupt, loud world. My parents always painted the picture of why we don't do this or that instead of just saying we don't. I saved myself for my husband because my mom took me to dinner on my fourteenth birthday and gave me a promise ring, explaining a beautiful picture of what marriage is and how God created it. She could have easily said "sex is bad, so don't do it" as a lot of parents do, but do you seriously think those words will keep your child when they are in love and have every teenage hormone racing through their body? Don't be naive. I am forever grateful to my mom for being willing to have those "awkward" talks so I didn't feel alone and left to figure those topics out on my own. Now my marriage is awesome, and I absolutely love being married. My parents' example and Mom's words of wisdom have forever impacted my marriage.

Thanks to my amazing parents and a relationship with Jesus, I have been saved from a lot of the heartache and pain the world brings. I know what it looks like to be a wife to my husband, and to be a fun, laid-back mom to my daughter and future children. I know that wherever God calls me to, He will provide a way. Nobody is perfect, and my parents made mistakes as do I, but if you lean on God and do your best, your children will be sharing about your legacy one day as well.

Homegrown Values and Fun

EDUCATING THE WHOLE PERSON

"The philosophy of the schoolroom in one generation will be the philosophy of government in the next."

ABRAHAM LINCOLN

God gives us the responsibility to raise and train our families in the way they should live. You can delegate some of that responsibility as long as you're watching whom you delegate it to *and* you play an active part in that process. If you don't know what your child is being taught and you're not a part of your child's education, your child could be fed a diet of poison. The old saying "An ounce of prevention is worth a pound of cure" holds true in no greater way than a child's training.

The goal of education is simple. Carolyn Cane says it best:

> If I learn my ABCs and can read 600 words
> per minute but have not been shown how to

communicate with the Designer of all language, I have not been educated.

If I have memorized addition facts, multiplication tables, and chemical formulas but have not been disciplined to hide God's Word in my heart, I have not been educated.

If I can recite the Gettysburg Address and the Preamble to the Constitution but have not been informed of the hand of God in the history of our country, I have not been educated.

If I graduate with a perfect 4.0 and am accepted at the finest university with a full scholarship but have not been guided into a career of God's choosing for me, I have not been educated.

However, if one day I see the world as God sees it and come to know Him, whom to know is life eternal, and glorify God by fulfilling His purpose for me, then I have been educated.

That should be our goal as parents, to choose the route of education and child training that will best achieve that destination. However you choose to educate your children, the most important consideration behind education is bringing them up in the knowledge and the reverence for God and His Word as truth.

A Different Route

We originally planned to sacrifice financially to put our kids in the best private Christian schools. When it came time to put Amy in school, I chose a highly reputed Christian school with an all-day kindergarten program. Since we were a close-knit family, our family felt torn apart without her and missed her every day. Every morning Tim would say, "Mom, where's Addie?" He called her "Addie" for some reason instead of Amy. "Where's Addie? I miss Addie! When is she coming home?"

Gary had wanted me to homeschool her, but I had concerns that I may be too impatient or get frustrated trying to teach. When Amy came home upset several days, telling me how the teacher yelled at the class, slamming things on her desk, I thought, *I can do that myself and not pay tuition for it! Even if I occasionally lose it, I care more about her than any teacher.* There was also a serious discipline issue with a troubled boy in the class, too. Amy would come home exhausted and tired as a little kindergartener, too tired to even play. Play and imagination are one of the most effective forms of learning.

> However you choose to educate your children, the most important consideration behind education is bringing them up in the knowledge and the reverence for God and His Word as truth.

By Christmas, I thought, *There's something wrong with this picture. This isn't the way it was meant to be—families being ripped apart. These kindergarteners are gone from home the same amount of time as working a full-time job!* Over the break I watched my son and daughter once again laughing and playing and being children, and I was moved deeply.

Around that time, we had a call from a business associate whose family was in trouble. They told us, "Our kids don't want to be around us. Our daughter makes us drop her off down the street from the school. They don't want to go anywhere with us, and our son struggles with a drug addiction. If we could do it all over, we wouldn't have put them in a public school system." I had seen pictures of the children hugging their parents when they were young and innocent, and I knew this family had a close relationship at one time. It made me rethink going along with the crowd to educate our children!

During that Christmas break, God dealt with my heart. I asked myself, "Why is it that we try to push our children out the door so early? Why do we let the world tell us we're supposed to send our little ones off to institutions? Am I doing this because it's the right thing for my family, or because it's the socially acceptable thing to the world? Are we really supposed to make them sit in classrooms and act and learn the same, at the same time in the same way? There has to be a better way!"

Speaking with home-educating families, I discovered that they were completing the one and a half hours of formalized learning needed a day in the time it took me to drive Amy back and forth to school, and then time doing homework added on to that (not to mention repairing the exposure to negative influences). I was investing more time than they were, and their results were stellar. Their children had time to play and be kids. Many could afford music lessons and family learning excursions with the money they saved over private schools. I discovered there were literally thousands of curriculums, utilizing every media platform, and the best of all, that God had equipped me as a loving parent to train my children toward their natural bent. I studied the many people who had been home educated and found that scores of great leaders were trained this way.

There are many alternatives to putting your children in public school that I would recommend. Nowadays, your children can take classes from the comfort of your home through online programs. There is private schooling, parents' cooperative (co-op) classes, homeschooling, or you can do a combination of all of them. I know many families that put their child in one public or private school class and homeschooled them for the rest. They did this so their children could lead Bible studies at their school or be involved in sports and extracurricular activities. Depending on your current situation and time availability, I am confident you can find the education route that works best for your family. Whichever route you take, the important thing is that you stay active in your child's education.

I chose the homegrown route, homeschooling our five children, but I also added in co-op classes for some seasons to enhance their educational opportunities with specialized classes or when time constraints made it helpful. We used DVD programs, field trips, seminars, business meetings, mission trips, family vacations, and every opportunity we could to expose them to learning and further their education. Once they were reading, they were off and running, learning subjects as their interests were peaked and maintaining a steady diet of reading, writing, and arithmetic. It's about finding the balance that works for you and what works best for your children.

Homeschooling is not a one size fits all program, but I am a big advocate for the benefits home education brings, and I believe it was one of the best decisions we made with our children. Home education is an amazing endeavor and definitely an option I encourage you to explore open-mindedly. Interestingly enough, aspiring young athletes, Olympians, musicians, actors, prodigies, and the socially elite are more typically educated by tutors or parents. It is considered a privilege and opportunity, so don't let anyone look down on a commitment to home education if this is what you choose.

There's a quote I love from a homeschooler whom I'm sure you know—Albert Einstein. He said, "It is, in fact, nothing short of a miracle that the modern methods of instruction have not yet entirely strangled the holy curiosity of inquiry; for this delicate little plant, aside from stimulation, stands mainly in need of freedom. Without this, it goes to wrack and ruin without fail. It is a very grave mistake to think that the enjoyment of seeing and searching can be promoted by means of coercion and a sense of duty. To the contrary, I believe it would be possible to rob even a healthy beast of prey of its voraciousness, if it were possible, with the aid of a whip, to force the beast to devour continuously, even when not hungry."

It's true. The best time to learn is when you're curious and want to explore. When you coerce someone to learn something the way you want it done, when you want it done, in a set method of pressure and conformity, you lose the creativity. Add a classroom of children and one teacher to that equation, and your child is set to become what the system conforms him or her to be. You lose the gift. You lose the uniqueness. You lose what's in that person. Romans 12:2 says, "Do not be conformed to the pattern of the world, but be transformed by the renewing of your mind."

We've heard, "Train up a child in the way they should go, and when they're old, they will not depart from it." We believed all along that our kids did not have to depart from the things of God. Our children are a gift from God, and God commissioned us to raise them up in His ways. We would account to Him for their training. Remember, a student will become like his teacher when he is fully trained, so it mattered who taught our children and what they were teaching them. The Son of God was trained in His parents' home and the synagogue. He was about His Father's business at age twelve with no rebellious years as a teen.

George Washington Carver, who was homeschooled, said, "Education is the key to unlock the golden door of freedom." In the early years of our nation, homeschooling was the vintage approach to education. Many great people who have shaped our history, such as Abraham Lincoln, were homeschooled. In fact, families and community imparted most education until the turn of the twentieth century.

Every Child's Development Should Be Shaped to Them

There's such a short window of opportunity to develop your child. Nobody ever went to their grave saying, "I wish I would have spent less time with my children and family." No, it's never about more money or prestige. It's always about family and relationships, the love and the care and the laughter and the tears. You get the joy of teaching your child to walk, why not get to hear them read their first words?

> When you coerce someone to learn something the way you want it done, when you want it done, in a set method of pressure and conformity, you lose the creativity.

Over three million children are now homeschooling in this nation. The number of children being homeschooled in America has increased by seventy-five percent over the past fourteen years in all states, according to a report in the online journal *Education News.* Thirty years ago, there was a smaller group of us who were considered strange radicals. People thought we were from a different planet and that our kids would all be backward and have no social skills. The truth is that eighty percent of homeschooled children achieved individual scores above the national average. Eighty percent! Fifty-four percent achieved scores in the top quarter of the entire population. Home educators score 18–30 points higher on achievement tests. "The study also indicates that public school performance gaps between minorities and genders were virtually nonexistent among the homeschooled students who took the tests."[10] Homeschoolers are going into Ivy League institutions, and colleges everywhere are actively going after homeschoolers.

More important than academic scores, you have the opportunity to instill homegrown character into your children. Without character and vintage values, we are left with educated fools. But with character, a person has the wherewithal to obtain knowledge. The opportunity to teach them real-life lessons goes beyond math equations and chemistry. You can teach them how to love God and how to have respect for the country and for the family. You can put before them the vision of how to be a mom or dad, how marriage and family systems work, and how to buy groceries, purchase a home, and many other practical life skills missing in schools. You place a perspective in front of them that it's okay for families to spend time with one another and for mothers and daughters and fathers and sons to have close relationships.

By the time most children are in third grade, they've concluded that it's not cool to be around their siblings and that it's considered okay to put them down and mistreat them. After graduation, almost nowhere in society will people be segregated by age, so age segregation encourages demeaning others of differing ages, whereas most home-educated children have a protective attitude toward the younger. Many children experience emotional or physical abuse in the school system. They are called names, put down, and creativity is diagnosed with labels such as ADD and other labels for children who learn differently.

Children do learn differently. I had to teach each of my children differently, because they all have their own unique personalities. Amy and Kirsten loved homework and learning; I could give them a book and they were fine reading it. Polly, however, disliked reading, and earlier on I had a hard time getting her to read books. When we were in a gift shop at the Grand Canyon, Polly spotted one of the first books she ever asked to read, *Over the Edge: Deaths in Grand Canyon*. Although it was slightly morbid, I was happy Polly showed interest in a book. She read that book cover-to-cover on our drive home, proudly sharing the interesting short stories with us. As a toddler, she always liked telling me a story instead of me telling her a story. Polly was fine with school, but it had to be presented to her in a different way than to Amy or Kirsten. I learned how to teach Polly in her learning style, and she graduated as valedictorian of her college class, a good lesson that children blossom at different times.

Tim, our second oldest, was a hands-on learner. To this day he loves house projects and building cabinets, and anything he can do with his hands. I was more effective with teaching Tim if I could give him something he could experience rather than reading the facts in a book, so with science I tried to include experiments and things he could try out for himself. He had a speech impediment when he was a little boy. I truly believe if I had put him in the school system, his self-esteem would have suffered greatly. A few simple lessons I used from a speech pronunciation book mixed with encouragement and prayer helped him. Today, Tim is preaching and teaching to youth weekly and thousands of adults on weekends. He doesn't have a speech impediment. He has an anointing and a calling of God on his life and is an amazing singer and songwriter.

Tom, our second son, was always very excited and energetic. If he had been put in the school system, I don't doubt he would have been wrongfully diagnosed ADD and put on Ritalin. Tom isn't ADD; he is creative. He loved to make things and run around on adventures. Every time we'd go somewhere, whether it was the mountains in Colorado or in our backyard, Gary would be saying, "Tom, stay away from the edge! Tom, stay with us!" Tom is now an amazing drummer, singer, songwriter/writer, and TV producer. He has created some unbelievable works, including a stage production that brought hundreds of teenagers to Christ. He didn't need to fit the mold; God created him uniquely for his purpose.

Protect Your Children Emotionally and Spiritually

More important than protecting your children emotionally, you need to protect them spiritually. Children are unstable as they grow up, easily persuaded and affected. It is a crucial time for spiritual growth, and it can also be a dangerous time for negative messages and attitudes to be planted in their hearts. Some things may be out of your control, but you have more influence and opportunity than you may think, so be mindful of protecting your children spiritually.

Pain seeks pleasure. When kids are told they can't do something special, and they're told that their uniqueness has to be put away and they have to be a clone of somebody else, they're in pain. They're hurt. They're boxed in and shut up. They can't be the person God designed them to be. When that happens, they get into trouble. They're looking for a way to act up, because they don't have anybody to encourage them!

When we were considering homeschooling our children, I asked myself, "God, what will they miss? I'm afraid they're going to miss out on sports, on prom, on this and that." I was praying because I knew homeschooling was a calling and a commitment. It is one of the most challenging jobs I've ever done, but it's also the most rewarding assignment that God's given me. Next to getting born again and filled with the Spirit, and marrying the right man, home educating my children has been the best decision I've ever made.

When I was asking God what my kids would miss, the Holy Spirit clearly said to me, "Your children are going to miss intense pressure toward premarital sex and multiplied partners. They're going to miss many opportunities to do drugs and drink alcohol. They're going to miss daily emotional abuse from peers and teachers who don't love them as you do and understand their giftings. They won't mold them into and develop them into the person whom I've called them to be."

I said, "God, I sign up. I'll take the job!"

And you know what? My children *have* missed all of those things, and your kids can miss those things, too. And we found great sports programs, formals, and created lots of fun and parties, so they didn't miss out on any fun. The Bible says your children don't have to depart before they choose God. They don't have to go away and make serious mistakes that they'll spend the rest of their lives trying to make right. They can take the path that God intended from the beginning.

> More important than protecting your children emotionally, you need to protect them spiritually.

That doesn't mean that they'll be perfect and always do it right. But when my kids messed up, I had the great joy of being there as their mom to embrace them, sometimes to discipline them, to love them, hug them, and tell them they can do better. I got to wipe away their tears, believe in them, and remind them that God believes in them. I got to be the one to tell them, "You can do it. I believe in you." I got to tell my daughters they're beautiful. I walked with my children through their first disappointments and times their friends hurt them. To be able to be there in those moments is greater than any academic achievement they could ever accomplish. The world has been our classroom, and the best part was we did it together.

I'll never forget the day when Tom came up to me and said, "When I grow up, Mommy, I'm going to marry you." A mom can't hear a better compliment than that!

The time I've had with my children is more precious than any career I could have had or anything else I could have done. I am so glad I did not give someone else the opportunity to take my children and mold them in the way they wanted. It is your job to place the vision of God in front of your children. You can either push your children away, or you can embrace the short nineteen to twenty years you have them in your home to impart into their lives. Whether that means staying involved in your children's education, homeschooling, or valuing every minute you can spend as a family, take hold of that and lead your family.

When we started home education, we were just going to do it for a few years and then enroll them in school. I had learned that home education could make a great impact on your child if you did it for the first three years of school. So when Amy was in third grade, I took her back to the Christian academy. They tested her for placement, and then the principal met with me. He said, "She's scoring on an eighth-grade level! She seems very happy. You seem to be doing well. What is your reason to put her in here?"

I was shocked. I said, "I thought I was supposed to."

> Homeschooling gives you a firsthand opportunity to see that your children have the best chance at successful living. Innocence is a delicate flower, and it's our job as parents to protect it in the home.

He leaned over to me and whispered, "Between you and me, what you're doing is really working. I would keep doing it if I were you!" I will always be grateful for his honesty and willingness to put my child's heart and education over a school's need to fill quotas. We kept putting off any other options year after year until we decided to homeschool until all of our children entered college.

Amy went to Christian college at sixteen years of age, and it was my first time adjusting to taking my child to school and dropping her off for an entire year. I was concerned about Amy adjusting okay, but the university's Dean of Students said to me, "Don't worry about her, she'll do fantastic. The home-educated kids do excellent. No worries." He was right. She landed the lead role in the college musical and aced her classes. The school tried to recruit her further to become an instructor, but she had other desires.

But home education only works if the model is right. You have probably seen varying results in different home-educated children. An occasional kid may be socially awkward, but most are hardworking and outgoing. There are a few stereotypically negative images of homeschoolers (and many negative of the public school crowd, too), and on the other hand, many businesses personally seek out homeschoolers for employees. Why is there such a dramatic difference?

My son Tim said it best. "Mom, I think home education is awesome, and I am so thankful you and Dad committed your time to home educating us. One thing I've learned, though, is that home education is the quickest way to replicate exactly who you are in your kids." It's true! I want to say that disciplining your children starts with disciplining yourself. I committed to grow as a person while I helped my children grow and learn, too. We both received an education in character, academics, and faith. We are replicating what we do in our children. Lest this frighten you, remember, the same holds true for the teachers and curriculums in the school system, and God knows what they're replicating!

So we need to be the right example. If you scream and yell and lose your temper all of the time, your children will copy that. If you make excuses for wrong behavior, your children will copy that. If you manipulate, your children will copy that. If you betray, your children will learn betrayal. If you're lazy, they will likely be, too. And no matter if your children are in the public school system or learning at home, they are going to learn something from your example.

Home education doesn't promise a foolproof method that your child will not make some mistakes or that you won't. People single out home-educated kids when one goes astray, but there are far more casualties and atrocities from the public education coffers. Homeschooling does, however, give you a firsthand opportunity to see that your children have the best chance at successful living. Innocence is a delicate flower, and it's our job as parents to protect it in the home.

Hiking the peaks for one of the most stunning views.

Learning is more fun on-site!

Do you feel that you are currently involved in the education of your children?

....

....

....

....

....

Have you noticed the difference in the personalities of your children through their unique way of learning?

....

....

....

....

....

Luke 6:40 says that a student will be like his teacher. Are you content with the role models and teachers your child has before them?

....

....

....

....

....

What can you take away from this chapter and apply to your life?

....

....

....

....

....

PART 4

The Vintage Legacy

NAVIGATING TO THE FINISH LINE

Tim's big day
with Best Man
Tom at his side.

All dressed up! Polly, Amy,
& Kirsten enjoying a winter
formal dance at church.

Polly marries her childhood crush, Jon.

Finalizing the Portrait

PARENTING TEENS

> "Families are the compass that guides us.
> They are the inspiration to reach great heights,
> and our comfort when we occasionally falter."
>
> BRAD HENRY

I was somewhat of a wreck in my teen years. Although I had good grades and an appearance of togetherness, I was the broken, insecure young girl who looked for love in all of the wrong places. I believed whatever propaganda the culture told me and lost myself trying to find myself in what I thought would deem me valuable. That took me down a dark road. Later in my teens, I found a relationship with God and started to work my way out of my mess. I discovered that the same zeal and longing that had gotten me into trouble apart from God could also help me piece my life back together with Him. That is why I love working with teenagers. They have the capacity and passion that we need; and we have the wisdom they need. We need one another.

If it wasn't for a few Christians who believed in the younger generation and were willing to mentor me, I would be far from where I am today. I am eternally grateful for the people who reached out to me during such a pivotal time in my life, and being able to do the same for others is a great opportunity.

Parenting teens has gotten such a bad reputation that it frightens some parents into wishing their little children could stay young forever. Instead of the teen generation receiving the aid they need to grow into godly men and women of God, they've been given labels to work through and distanced from the mentorship they need. People don't talk about the great reward or how much fun parenting a teenager is; rather, they make statements such as "I'm sure your mom is glad to have a break from you" or "I bet your parents can't wait for school to start again." Those words have negative effects on youth, and ill-intended remarks or labels can shape their mindset at that age.

The same goes for mothers. When I was raising my children, more experienced mothers would approach me and say, "Your children are so well behaved." My heart would heave a sigh of relief, because when you're in the trenches of parenting, sometimes you need encouragement to refuel your will to fight. Then they would add, "Wait until they're teenagers and rebel against you."

Why do people make those kinds of negative statements? I do know that miserable people enjoy spreading misery. Some parents who experienced hardship justify themselves by putting their mistakes on others. You don't have to accept that prediction as your truth. I had the most fun with my children in their teen years. We travelled together and were able to do things that we couldn't when they were young. None of them rebelled. When you do it God's way, you're not going to get the same results as the world's system.

The goal in parenting is to train and mentor your children and teenagers for life. A teenager is dealing with new aspects in their mind, will, and emotions as they go through puberty and start hearing different messages at school. Your teen needs you to understand the changes that are happening and mentor them through it, because those are all major factors in their life.

In the middle school years, your children are looking for heroes, and they want you to be that hero. Establish and keep a close relationship with them. Invest time into your teens. Be the one who gives them the answers they need; don't leave them to find those answers in the wrong places. Don't direct them to their peers and the Internet to find out how life is supposed to be lived. What you should desire as a parent is that if your child has a question about life, about sex, about relationships, they can come and freely talk to you. Create an open environment of communication where they don't feel that you're going to judge them or get angry with them for bringing those questions to you.

A lot of parents treat their teenagers as though they're small children. That insults the teenager's process of becoming an adult, and the teen will resent the parent. Teenagers can't simply be told something is wrong and be sent to their room; teenagers need you to talk out mistakes and build that relationship with them. You have to bring the "why" alongside the dos and don'ts. You have to start testing them with responsibility. And if they start a discussion with you and you don't agree with their position, don't turn it into an argument and get emotional. Teenagers need to talk things out, and arguing shuts off the communication. Instead, use it as a teaching moment. Sometimes they want to hear an explanation because they are trying to figure out the "why" behind the "what," and that's very normal.

If your teenager asks you, "Why is this a sin?" don't panic. Don't shut them down. Look at it as an honest question and give them the "why" behind the "what."

As parents, when we look at our teenagers, we see these tall bodies and grown-up faces, and we expect them to act that way.

The problem is, they are still on the process to becoming an adult. Inside, they're still kids! They're still just trying to figure everything out! We see the physical changes, but there are still emotional and spiritual changes occurring in them. They still need security. They still need boundaries. They're not ready to take on the world. They still need you to be their parent.

Boundaries and Hormones

There are two main components you're dealing with as you parent through the teen years. The first is *boundaries*. Many people believe they should let their teenagers experiment as to not risk being overbearing and scaring them off, but it's just the opposite. This a very insecure time for teens as so many things change and everything in their world is shaken. Their body changes, they begin to be drawn to the opposite gender, their skin starts breaking out, and they may feel awkward or clumsy. There's a lot of peer pressure to conform. You need to set boundaries that are going to protect your teens and give them security.

> Your teen needs you to understand the changes that are happening and mentor them through it, because those are all major factors in their life.

Technology has added a whole new complexity factor to boundaries, but there are tools available and rules you can set in place to help monitor and protect your children. I recommend not allowing children to have laptops or cell phones in their room at night, and it's better to have a stationary desktop that your children use that is near a place you frequent often. My children all shared one stationary desktop right by our laundry room and Gary's office for many years. You can also purchase programs for computers that put a lock on websites with adult content and that can track all movement on a computer or cell phone for you to see. It's important to remember that smart phones can access the Internet as well. Set boundaries on technology use and monitor those boundaries.

Boundaries should be less focused on small issues and chiefly focused on establishing honesty, character, respect, and integrity in a child.

The second component is *hormones.* As your children reach their teens, the culture and peer pressure are driving them toward sex. That's why Gary and I didn't let our children date when they were in their early teens. If they aren't in the season of marriage, why would we subject our children to the heartbreak and peer pressure that can come with dating? And where is a relationship between thirteen-year-olds who are going through puberty going to lead to, anyway? Not anywhere good!

Protect your child's awakening of romantic love, as it says to do in Song of Solomon 8:4 NLT: "Promise me, O women of Jerusalem, not to awaken love until the time is right."

In fact, our children took a different approach to dating altogether. Our children became friends with the person first and got to know them outside of a romantic relationship. Our family got to know them as well. And as the relationship progressed, there were boundaries in place. That's principally what courtship is about—putting boundaries in place to protect a relationship and each person in the relationship. The intent of courtship is that a person reserves their affection and sexual intimacy for the person they marry. As a result, both people should be in a season of marriage and have an established friendship before entering into a relationship. They should also be committed to marriage as a potential, if not probable, outcome *before* they take the next step of courting. Accountability is there for the couple. We didn't leave our children alone in situations where they could be tempted.

Courtship has a reputation of being old-fashioned, and indeed it was the vintage approach to marriage until the sexual revolution. My husband's grandparents, Chester and Gladys, courted each other by spending time with family or a church group. Their beautiful marriage lasted their lifetime. Many parents think it's impossible for teens to wait for sex until marriage, but it's more than possible and even used to be the standard. It comes down to training. Chester and Gladys were trained to abstain from sex until marriage, just as the majority of teens today are trained toward premarital sex.

Moving a relationship slowly through stages of development and abstaining from sex till marriage has a proven track record of lower divorce rates and higher levels of marital commitment. A rush-to-sex-without-investment mentality results in higher divorce rates and lower levels of sexual satisfaction once married. You can still adopt the valuable principles in courtship and adapt it to dating or simply waiting on true love. It's about honoring each other and God's plan for marriage, and that never goes out of style. You've heard the saying, "Don't throw the baby out with the bathwater," right? The same holds true here. Don't throw out the vintage values that could improve your life just because you don't like the package that they come in. Repackage them in a way that works for you!

Our son-in-law Jason came on staff at our ministry, and around two months later someone who was also working in our ministry tipped me off that he was going to ask me if he could get to know my daughter Amy outside of work. When this staff member first told me, I said "absolutely not," because we hardly knew him, but then I paused. "You've known him for six years. What would you say if you were me?"

"Well," she said, "he's the most loving person I've ever met, and he has the most character of any man I've known. If she were my daughter, I would absolutely be all over it."

I dropped a hint to Amy to see if she would be interested—and she was. So Jason nervously approached me and asked if he could see Amy outside of work. He shared his intentions and his feelings for Amy. He felt that God had opened a lot of doors in order for them to meet, and I agreed. He waited patiently for my reply, both terrified and excited.

"I would have said no," I started, "but I've checked out your character. I already did the background check." I winked. "You can get to know Amy outside of work if that's what she wants, but you'll have to do so by coming to our home. We're off on Mondays and Sunday evenings. We usually hang-out as a family and maybe pop some popcorn and watch a movie. You can come over on those days, if that's what you want."

> Courtship has a reputation of being old-fashioned, and indeed it was the vintage approach to marriage until the sexual revolution.

Many men would have backed out there, but Jason agreed. He didn't complain or get angry. He said, "Yes, ma'am!" And he started coming and hanging out with our family. He showed us his character right off, and he has proven that character again and again throughout their marriage. He is a wonderful father to their two children and a great son-in-law to us.

Our world's dating culture has produced a "try it before you buy it" practice, resulting in less commitment and higher divorce statistics (not to mention premarital sex, unwanted pregnancies, and abortions). That is the message being communicated to teenagers. I was surprised when my teens received pressure from adults to give up their beliefs and "try it before you buy it." One couple asked my daughter, "How will you know you really like him if you haven't slept with him?" The standards even the older generation are setting for the younger generation are ridiculous. The message: "Have sex, drink, do drugs, live your life while you're young, and you won't have any consequences or regrets" is abhorrent to me because the opposite is true. Having worked with teens in ministry and dealt with the aftermath, I know what a deception that is.

The individuals involved are the biggest contributing factors to the success in any relationship. A proper understanding of the goal of courtship and the maturity of those involved are crucial to success. It's easier to blame one method or another for our own mistakes, other people's mistakes, selfishness, or misunderstandings rather than examining our own hearts. That is why boundaries are crucial, because we're all human and all prone to making the wrong choices without accountability.

We painted a picture for our children that intimacy was an amazing thing that God created for marriage. Passion is awesome, but it must be for the right person and for the right time.

The "Sex" Talk

One of the frequent questions I receive is, "How and when do you talk to your children about sex?" With a society that has few moral boundaries left and no restraint for protecting a child's heart from adult topics, we *must* be the ones who introduce these discussions with our children, and unfortunately for the same reasons, at increasingly earlier ages. The exact age will depend on the environment you create for your children and their exposure to secular training in the school systems. I encourage parents to set the stage for openness very early in life so that your children see you as their source for information and not their school or peers.

I learned the facts of life from reading the curse word of all curse words on the elementary bathroom wall in the third grade. I asked another girl what it meant. She volunteered the graphic information to my horror. Because I had no idea where the conversation would go, I carried some serious guilt and wrong perceptions for too many years.

It's sad to think that one of the most impactful areas of marriage would be introduced to a child by a stranger or worse yet, a system that does not recognize God's rapturous plan for marriage or sex between one man and one woman. I won't even go into the horrible presentations and considerations being propagated to small children in the school system today. These designs come from those who deplore God's design for family and have done everything in their power to corrupt and destroy the simple purity and organic beauty of sexual intimacy. Too many children are being introduced to sex through exposure to pornography—another good reason not to allow technology outside of your supervision.

> We painted a picture for our children that intimacy was an amazing thing that God created for marriage. Passion is awesome, but it must be for the right person and for the right time.

Innocence should have a place once again in the tenderness of childhood. Guard your child's heart from sitting under the mentorship of thieves and carefully tend to your child's heart by sharing truth before someone tells them a lie!

Children should not be made to feel shame concerning their sexual organs. I encourage you to use the appropriate names for these areas so later it will be easier to explain reproduction. It is also necessary to explain and help children understand, "These are special hidden parts that we don't show to people or let others touch. Tell me if anyone tries to touch your special parts." You can create your own positive wording.

Introduce children to reproduction by casual mentions in daily life from the time they are small children, but don't take information into conversations past their curiosity or appropriateness. A five-year-old may ask, "Where do babies come from?" A simple explanation such as, "Mommies and daddies make babies," may suffice. If they ask, "How do they do that?" you can escalate to the next level. "They both give something from their love to make the baby" could take it a step further. "The mommy gives an egg and the daddy gives a sperm" may be the follow up.

> It is important to give them an understanding of "the gift" of sexual intimacy that is intended by God as a wedding present to the one they will marry.

Often simple explanations are enough for their understanding at early ages. Referring to a mommy's pregnant belly as where the baby is also let's children begin to understand reproduction. Eventually this conversation can keep going until through a natural process over time, the information they need is covered.

Some children have more curiosity and will continue to ask until they are satisfied. One of our sons was riding in the car with me at age ten and asked every question possible until he had the entire basic understanding. It wasn't awkward and it was unplanned (at least in my mind). One of the reasons I am such an advocate of home education is that you can't always plan these times, so you're grateful that quantity time offers a better opportunity for mentorship in quality time.

During adolescence, take this conversation to a place of understanding of the changes that will start occurring in their body as they grow into adults. Discuss menstrual cycles and bodily changes before they happen to your child. Dads should address the negative influence of pornography, handling temptations, and the importance of honoring God and women. Again, if you talk about this beforehand, you are established as the "go-to" person for answers in this delicate area. I recommend that dads have these talks with their sons consistently and moms with their daughters if possible. It doesn't always work that way as in my son's situation. If you're a single mom, you can handle this with the help of God's Spirit guiding you (age dependent on their innocence and environment), and maybe the help of a trusted godly man in your son's life.

Beyond adolescence in your child, I encourage you to share all the information in this chapter. Help guide your youth to make a commitment with God's help to maintain a pure heart and physically abstain from sexual intimacy or encounters until marriage. Some families follow these talks with a ring, certificate, or other reminder of their desire and commitment to follow God's plan of waiting until marriage for sexual intimacy.

It is important to give them an understanding of "the gift" of sexual intimacy that is intended by God as a wedding present to the one they will marry. If a couple models marriage as this writing encourages, children should have a healthy picture of the relationship and will want to save the gift of sex for their future mate. Asking questions such as, "Do you want your future spouse to save this gift for you? Do for them as you would like them to do for you. You can also pray for this person now, that they would learn to honor and obey God in this area, too."

I was a youth minister for nine years, and during that time I had the opportunity to encourage parents about leadership and communication, but I was surprised that many parents would not address sex with their youth. It became such a concern that

I eventually decided to teach the scriptural and physical aspects of the "marriage bed" with the older teens and their parents. I did so with the girls in our home with their mothers present. My husband did the same with the boys at a camp out with their fathers present.

Our thought was we could break the ice for parents scripturally, and this would turn the discussion over to their parents to continue. We made our intentions clear through invitations, letters, and signed releases that we were having this discussion and that it was important for a parent to attend if possible. Unfortunately, less than half of the parents attended, but they sent their youth.

Parents must reclaim their right and responsibility to be the voice in their children's lives. This is a vintage value. Churches can only go so far in the spiritual leadership of your children, but God holds you personally accountable. Do not delegate this role to a school system.

God's Gift of Sex

Following are some of the discussions I shared with my children and encourage you to have about God's gift of sex with your youth. By the way, abstaining from premarital sex is not just for girls, but God gives His Word to young men for their best, too.

The marriage act is awesome and beautiful. God made sex. He is not a prude, and He is not trying to hurt you or keep you from fun by telling you to save sex only for marriage. There are important reasons to keep sex for marriage. Sex is so much more than two people sharing an act. Sex is a gift from a loving God who made us male and female. He gave us this gift, and we give it to our future spouse.

He gave us the opportunity to share in the creation of a child, which is also the highest purpose for marriage according to Malachi 2:15, "Why did God make the two one, because he sought a godly seed." Having sex with multiple people is an attack on God's plan for children and family life, as is evidenced by the brokenness in our culture today.

When two people have sex together, they are becoming "one" physically, but also one in a spiritual union as well. Sex is a spiritual act as well as a physical act. The act of sex creates a phenomenal bond to be shared at the highest level of closeness and intimacy with one person for a lifetime. It is an act of gift-giving to each other. Sex is not just for the pleasure of one person or the other, but it should be a mutually enjoyable exchange for both male and female.

When people share this bond with several people, it makes the act become common. It damages the intimacy a person is able to experience by hardening a person's heart. It hurts each person and creates wounds so deep in the heart that no psychologist can unravel the pain (God can, however). People who have multiple sex partners wrestle to stay in lifelong marriages. Statistically, those who have multiple sex partners or premarital sex have a much greater incidence of divorce. If a person struggles to honor marriage by exercising personal restraint before marriage, they will most likely struggle to stay committed and exercise personal restraint once married.

Both single persons and married persons have to exercise self-control and discipline to remain faithful. Being married doesn't mean you will not have temptations to be unfaithful after marriage, so start learning self-control by God's Spirit now as a single person.

Sex is the seal of a marriage covenant. Covenants are not contracts. A contract is easily torn up or broken, but covenants are not. In a contract, two people agree to be in the relationship until the other person does something they don't like, but in a covenant, both parties agree to hold up their end whether or not the other party does. God made a covenant with us when He sent Jesus to save us from our sin. When we accept Him as our Savior, we enter into a blood covenant. His blood covers our sin.

Marriage is a covenant between a man and a woman that God joins together. Jesus said, "What God has joined together, let no man separate." God is the witness to the covenant commitment between couples on their wedding day. The Bible says that God acts as a witness between you and your covenant partner.

Sex is the consummation or the physical oath to that covenant, which is a lot more serious than a one-night stand or the casual attitude our world has about sex! Regardless of how a person chooses to change this view or definition does not change God's view.

God says that marriage is a mystery or allegory that models the relationship between Christ and the Church. Jesus made a covenant with His blood, shedding it to lay His life down for us, to redeem us, to make us holy. We received His perfect record, and He bore our mistakes and our less than perfect record by giving Himself up for us on the cross. This is how a man should love his wife, laying his life down to protect and provide for her, and the wife should respond with her respect and honor.

This makes the instruction to couples clearer from Ephesians 5:25–33 ESV:

> Husbands, *love your wives, as Christ loved the church* and *gave himself* up for her, that he might sanctify her, having cleansed her by the washing of water with the word, so that he might present the church to himself in splendor, without spot or

wrinkle or any such thing, that she might be holy and without blemish. In the same way husbands should *love their wives as their own bodies.* He who loves his wife loves himself. For no one ever hated his own flesh, but nourishes and cherishes it, just as Christ does the church, *because we are members of his body.* "Therefore a man shall leave his father and mother and hold fast to his wife, and *the two shall become one flesh."* This *mystery is profound,* and I am saying that *it refers to Christ and the church.* However, let each one of you *love his wife as himself,* and let the wife see that *she respects* her husband.

Sex is a holy act to God, and therefore should be to us as well. It is a celebration of marriage and a gift of joy. When a man gives himself to his wife and she gives herself to him sexually, the penis penetrates her hymen (in the vagina) and causes a small shedding of blood. Many believe that this shedding of blood is yet another symbolic portrayal of Christ shedding His blood, giving Himself for the church. Jesus was willing to die for His church, and a husband is to love his wife with this same kind of giving, covenant love.

This may help us understand in a greater way why there's so much attack to dishonor the plan of marriage and to desecrate the holy beauty of sex. A Focus on the Family post, "Reflecting Our Relationship with God" by David Kyle Foster[11], has this to say:

And so we see why Satan is so intent in defacing and destroying human sexuality and marriage. He is trying to mock God. He is trying to mar the very image of God expressed on this earth through the marital bond, sexual and otherwise. He is trying to rob God of His deepest and most passionate intention—that of marital union with man—because if he can destroy the beauty of the earthly bond, he can destroy in us any desire for the heavenly bond.

You and I, and every believer, were created to live in marital union with God, both now and in the age to come. Everything about a healthy marital union on this earthly plane has been designed by God to be a reflection of the interaction that we are meant to have with God Himself:

- the covenant that is struck to bind us together eternally;
- the signs and symbols of that covenant that are a public declaration of that bond;
- the keeping pure of oneself for the other;
- the wedding party, with a host of invited guests looking on, rejoicing in the display of our mutual love and affection;
- intimate moments of sharing our deepest self with the other, resulting in new life being born and a oneness of body, soul, and spirit;
- over time, the development of a oneness of heart that produces a unity of thinking, and even, appearance (Romans 8:29; 2 Corinthians 3:18; 1 John 3:2—"when He appears, we shall be like Him").

The parallels are endless.

In sharing this concept of purity with youth, it is important to share that the same blood that Christ shed for our sins can cleanse us of any impurities and sins we may have committed in the area of sexual immorality. If you or your young person has messed up in this area or another, it is in no way God's desire for you to feel condemned. We have all sinned and fallen short of God's best in one way or another. The only thing that can cleanse and restore us is God's love and Jesus' sacrifice for our lives. Receive His transformational love and power in your life, marriage, and relationships. Let God restore what Satan has attempted to steal in your life or that of your child. Always extend love and mercy to your child. God's love is greater than any error. Mercy triumphs over judgment.

> Marriage is a covenant between a man and a woman that God joins together.

As parents, our greatest desire is to spare our children pain and to aid them in making good decisions before they would fall into a well-laid trap of the culture that is attempting to drive an agenda using children as pawns. Even the strongest of families struggle to be watchful over the sexually charged deluge of messages, and some families have fallen into unsuspecting error. These errors can occur if we present life and sexual intimacy from a legalistic standpoint, creating rebellion in the strong-willed or fear in the timid. Your intent should never be to incite fear in a child, but instead to *create a vision* for something greater. A child can more easily say yes to eating broccoli if they know dessert is coming! The law of sin and death brings death, but the law of life in Christ Jesus brings freedom.

Give your children a picture of *the gift* of marriage and the *why* to save sexual intimacy for their future mate. I do believe this also includes an understanding of honoring God and His design. That vision should start in our own homes and how we treat our marriage.

Don't Forget the Temptations

We can't be naive when it comes to youth and hormones. Don't forget the temptations lauding themselves on every newsstand, computer screen, and television program, trying to entrap your son or daughter. My husband had monthly and sometimes weekly discussions with each of our sons to ask them how they were doing in this area. We once left a vacation resort in Riviera Maya because the Spanish tourists were topless (and almost bottomless), and the resort refused to uphold their policies concerning this. Our sons said, "We don't want to be here. Let's leave!"

What is not talked about in a healthy way can become a dirty little secret. There are increasing issues in homes between siblings, especially step-siblings, concerning sexual exchanges. Just because they are brothers or sisters doesn't exempt them from temptations, especially when the seeds are being planted constantly from the time a youth wakes, attends a secularized, sexualized school with hormonal peers and sexual taunts, checks their smartphone thirty to forty times an hour, turns on the television, works on a computer with pop-ups, and goes to adulterated movies. That's a ton of sexual messaging!

I had a young girl tell me that no adult could withstand that kind of pressure, so how did her parents expect her to since they put her in the school? This was a youth begging me to ask her parents to homeschool her!

Acquaint your youth with the story of King David's son Amnon and how he lusted for his half-sister, Tamar (2 Samuel 13). It clearly illustrates that what a young man thinks is love because of hormones can merely be lust. The Scripture says after he raped her, he hated Tamar as much as he loved her (or so he thought it was love). Love is a desire to give to a person, to bless and honor God's plan for them. Lust desires a person for what it can get from them; it uses them for self-gratification. Teach your youth the difference between lust and love. Amnon's sin cost his family great hardship, hatred, pain, and death.

A fireside worship time with girls at a youth camp turned into several confessions of struggles with pornography. Yes, girls are being bombarded with the same lustful, demonically charged lies and images, pop-ups, and porn, too. Lots of open communication can help children and youth sort through temptations and how to handle them.

> Don't forget the temptations lauding themselves on every newsstand, computer screen, and television program, trying to entrap your son or daughter.

Pray and communicate. I sometimes see critical blogs from youth who have rebelled, complaining that their parents taught them to save their body for marriage and that they were wrong to do so. Maybe their parents' methods lacked, or maybe the young person is simply defiant because they chose sin over God's plan, but their worst criticisms of purity or courtship teachings do not compare with the devastating results of the schools and the carnage of abortions, broken hearts, suicides, and breakdowns of "the system." So even if a few rebel against some of the concepts I've shared, for every rebel there are many more of those who have a loving marriage today with positive experiences that far outweigh the few who are bent on rebellion. Everyone will not agree with these vintage values, but they don't have to for them to be right. It's not my Word; it's God's.

Do you feel that you've set appropriate boundaries for your children?

....

....

....

....

....

What messages are being communicated to teenagers through media? Do you feel that they are positive or negative messages?

....

....

....

....

....

What are some areas you would like to see improvement with in your relationship with your teenager or in your boundaries set for your teenager?

....

....

....

....

....

What can you take away from this chapter and apply to your parenting?

....

....

....

....

....

Kirsten's MONOGRAPH

MY FIFTH BORN

My parents looked on with a mixture of amusement and sheer terror. They heard about what was happening; now they witnessed it with their own eyes. There I stood, a dead raccoon in my hands, barefoot in our poison ivy enclosed and mud prone woods. I was playing my own rendition of "survivor" in our woods with two friends—twenty-four hours overnight without a tent, with only the food my friends and I could savage from the great outdoors. We cooked up the raccoon and ate it. My dad shook his head in disbelief and said, "I'm a hunter, and this is too much for even *me*. I can't believe what I'm seeing."

My brother Tim shot the raccoon for us, and he had helped me shoot my first ever wildlife only minutes before as well. Our total diet for the twenty-four hours consisted of undercooked rabbit (my fault), two birds, and a fat raccoon. We had no seasoning salts, so unfortunately we had to taste the grit of real wildlife, and our hunger pains only mildly disguised the odd flavors. You're probably asking what would possess three teenage girls who are picky eaters and had probably never started a fire in our whole lives to play survivor and skin a raccoon without a second thought?

Two words: *bucket list.*

Being the youngest of my family with four siblings leading the way ahead of me, it's easy for me to feel like an old soul. I like to think of it like a rollercoaster. The front of the rollercoaster climbs over the hill slowly, but once it picks up momentum, that momentum pulls the back of the rollercoaster over the hill with surprising speed. And I'm the back of that rollercoaster! That's why I have a bucket list chock-full of crazy things that remind me to be young and daring, because nobody would do these things if they weren't. The best part is that I have a wonderful family that isn't too scared to try new things and is willing to experience life with me, so I never have to try these things alone.

My siblings are my best friends. Whether it's going over to Tim and Alecia's to go on a run and then binge eating all of the calories we burned after, playing video games all night with Tom and Tabitha, getting Chinese food and watching a movie with Polly and Jon, or playing baseball in the backyard with Amy and Jason, they are all always my preferred company. Many families grow apart with age, but I feel closer to my siblings now than I even did when we lived in the same house.

Many people have approached me over the years and asked, "What did your parents do different?" I never could find an answer that satisfied that question. I could say that it was their faithfulness to us children, or their contagious passion for God, or even the valuable principles they instilled in us growing up— all of those would be good answers, but those aren't *the* answer. I know a lot of people do those things for their children and their children still rebel against God.

I couldn't put my finger on it for the longest time, and then I realized what it was—my parents made life fun for us! My parents showed us that marriage and being a family could be fun and attractive, ministry could be fun, and serving God could be fun. It's not one specific principle or rule that makes my family so great, but it's the *environment* that my parents cultivated. That's why it has always been difficult for me to give a simple answer to that question.

When your family has fun together, it's an attractive quality. You can't help but want to be around that kind of environment. And when serving God is fun, can you imagine what that communicates to your children? My parents instilled that in us as children. We would wake up and find that we were going on a spontaneous trip somewhere, or we were going to our local rollercoaster park for the day. My family didn't just live together; *we did life together!* We went out and saw and experienced things as a family, and that's what we're still doing today.

My mom let us try new things. In fact, she was our cheerleader. If she knew that we wanted to do something, she would get behind that vision and believe in us even before we believed in ourselves. Vocal lessons, dance lessons, local play auditions—whatever it was, Mom would be right behind us saying, "You can do it! Don't give up now!" My mom operates in many roles in my life—friend, counselor, teacher, and supporter. She is the most courageous and inspiring woman I know, and I'm so thankful I get to call her Mom. I always know she's got my back.

I've dragged my beautiful mother on many of my escapades, and she goes along willingly. We went bungee jumping in New Zealand, skydiving in Australia, and most recently we toured Japan. It was always my dream to go to Japan, and yes, a bucket list item as well. My mother knew that, so she made it happen. A month before we went to Japan, I added "experience a safe earthquake" to my bucket list, and we got that in Tokyo. I was thrilled. Of course, my mom's first question was, "Why would you put an *earthquake* on your bucket list?" Well, all I can say is that kids will be kids!

I grew up with my dad telling all of us children stories, and I can remember how excited I would get when he'd start the theme song to one of his infamous ongoing storylines. All five of us children would try to squeeze on Mom and Dad's bed, and the unfortunate few who couldn't fit would pile on the floor. As the youngest, my spot was always reserved right by my dad. He'd tell us the latest mystery from our friend, the small mouse detective, who was always eluding large cats and flying his miniature helicopter to the safety of our barn where he lived. When the story was over, I'd beg my dad to tell us another one.

We would compete on the "Tootsie Roll Show" in the car, which was a game show my dad made up where he asked us science questions and we competed against other children around the world (who were all voiced by my dad). The game show prize was a "truck full of Tootsie Roll Pops delivered to your front yard," although I admit I only ever received a handful of them from the gas station when I won, which I carried around the house as if they were worth a million bucks. As time progressed, so did our adventures, and soon we were on to top secret mystery cases alongside private detectives.

> My family didn't just live together; we did life together! There is nothing more fun or more interesting to me than my family.

My dad and I would be on our way to church when he would make a ringing sound and pick up his phone. "Yes? Sure, Kirsten's here. What did they do this time?" He'd fill me in on the latest details of a new mystery. I grinned ear to ear as I faked phone calls with the FBI, using my hand as the phone. I caught the culprit every time, all over the course of a thirty-minute car ride. My dad and I had countless journeys like this. My dad is the most lovable and respect worthy man I know, and every car ride, story, and adventure we had together meant the world to me.

There is nothing more fun or more interesting to me than my family. My family and I have been swimming with eight-foot lemon sharks together in Bora Bora. I ran a Tough Mudder with my sister and brother, Polly and Tom, and their spouses, Jon and Tabitha, which involved twelve miles scattered with extreme obstacles. I don't ever need to go out searching in the wrong places for a good time, because any time with my family is the best time. It is a powerful thing when your children can turn to their church or to their family to have fun, instead of turning to the world's unsatisfying outlets, such as partying. I believe that's how God designed it to be.

My favorite family Christmas is the year when we had record levels of snow mounding outside, and the power went out due to the snowstorm. We were snowed in, with no electricity to play with our new toys and game systems. Everyone couldn't scatter to their corner of the house after opening their presents or isolate themselves with all of their new memorabilia. We all went up to one room in the house, hung a blanket over the doorway to keep the cool air out, and played games together as a family all day. Dad was able to light that one room with our generator. At night we laid our blankets next to one another, and before we went to sleep we watched a Christmas movie by the fireplace. I was around eight years old then, and every Christmas after that I prayed the power would go out again so we could relive that great Christmas.

That's what family is all about. It's about doing life together with the people you love. Your family life should be fun! Try new things, go to new places, and make new memories. Use what you have right now and build the best life you can build. Take the time to imagine with your children and believe in their dreams. Be their number one cheerleader. Tell stories. Have adventures. Show your children how to have good, old-fashioned fun with you, and that friendship will carry you through the harder times of training and mentorship.

Kirsten and I exploring Japan!

Gary with his Alaskan trail guide, Kirsten.

Feel Young Again

THE NEXT GENERATION

"Grandchildren are the dots that connect the lines from generation to generation."

LOIS WYSE

No preparation could really have prepared me to be a Grand-mama. Our firstborn, Amy, awarded me the tribute of being her maid of honor, and two and a half years later, she and Jason asked to deliver our first grandbaby in our home! I am no stranger to homebirths (another vintage approach), so I rejoiced that they had chosen this. What a special blessing to share our home for such a glorious occasion!

The day before Amy's water broke, she said, "I want to go to Red Lobster for dinner." Now that is my secret way to go into labor, and has been for years. It almost always worked. Sure enough, the following morning, Amy's water had leaked so she and Jason came on over, just in case labor kicked in.

For Saturday, Sunday, and Monday, we had fun waiting— we laughed and told stories from the kids' childhood days while

Amy peacefully breathed through a contraction here or there, danced to her father's piano music like we did when they were children, and visited and laughed with her sisters and brothers and me. There was peace, laughter, and no pressure.

Monday afternoon, we were all so grateful for the gift of time, to stop the busyness and be together before this life-changing event. Time stood still. I truly believe it was God's reward to us for being about His Kingdom. He always gives us just what we need when we need it. Now, we were ready! Amy stood on the trampoline and gently rocked. We took walks, and even a drive. On the drive, Monday evening, Amy felt pressure! Yes, I knew what that meant. We headed back ready for the transition to push. Four and a half hours later, Journey Taylor was born. Beautiful, alert, a head full of dark hair, with her little hand up in the air over her ear—it was like looking at Amy all over again, and we were all filled with tears of joy!

Amy was amazing in her resolve, peace, and womanhood. She was changed, and so were we. The mutual respect we had for each other and friendship had gone to another level and continues as I watch Amy lay her life down to be such an amazing mother.

I lost track of days and nights over the next week, as we coddled Journey, adjusted, and learned the baby's needs. As new daddy Jason said humorously, "We aren't parents, yet. Parents mentor and train, but we're the ones being trained by Journey." We laughed. All the memories of sleepless nights, trying to settle Amy to nurse, and changing diapers came back. Jason and Amy went to their home, and we had to say good-bye and go back to busy lives again.

Then the moment I had been waiting for came. They came back over for a visit. Amy rested for three hours to recover from missed sleep, while I held little Miss Journey. She fell asleep in my arms, and I dared not move, so I sat with my iPhone in hand on reverse picture mode, capturing and watching her every movement—awake, asleep, yawn, asleep again. As Journey was waking up contentedly, she turned her head and looked into my eyes. We gazed at each other. I was spellbound. She smiled! Yes, she did, honestly. I have the picture to prove it. Actually, I have fifty to prove it!

I was in love all over again. I started thinking of buying an RV to take her to see the world, just as we had dreamed with our own children. More thoughts, more dreams, more plans. Being a grandparent doesn't just change you; it gives you a rebirth, a revival!

On being a grandparent, Gary says, "My perspective in seeing a child is different today than from my chaotic days of just trying to survive when we had our own children. I didn't understand

> Recognize that what you feed a child's spirit has eternal consequences.

the sheer joy and priority of a child. I am thankful our children have a better grasp on family life and understanding than we had. I am also thankful to get the opportunity to experience the gift of a child all over again from a different perspective." If anyone tells you it's great to be a grandparent, don't believe them— it's better than that!

Gary and I did buy that RV the year Journey was born with visions of us stealing away with our grandchildren, introducing them to the vast world of national parks and road travel as we did with our children. We've taken a few trips with two of the couples and a grandbaby, but hopefully the best discoveries will come when they are a little older. I bought a sign and hung it in the RV that says, "Grandparents, so easy to control even a small child can do it!" We've already bought into the idea that we will let the grandchildren have pretty much what they want, "if it's OK with Mommy and Daddy."

Generational Relationships in the Balance

Once you reach the grandparent phase of family life, you realize what's important and what isn't. You also realize that so many of the issues and concerns you had with your own children were not as big of a deal as you thought, such as the age they have their first bite of something sweet or whether you use cloth or disposable diapers. I know about the arguments for both of these areas; I made them! The point is: "Don't miss the big picture!"

It's more important what you put in your child's or grandchild's spirit and soul than anything else. If you don't let them have any sugar until after a year and wash hundreds of cloth diapers to protect their skin, but fail to proactively feed them a steady diet of God's Word and power along with manners, morals, and church involvement, you will have missed the boat. Scriptures warn us that people choke on a gnat and swallow a camel. Recognize that what you feed a child's spirit has eternal consequences. Protect them from evil messaging while providing a diet of truth from God's Word. Of course, teach them to properly care for their body and feed it healthy, whole foods as much as possible.

You can feed a grandchild God's Word and pray for them daily. Spending time with your grandbaby early on and making a bond as soon and often as possible is essential to your lifelong relationship. The more respect you show to the parents, the more trust they will have toward you. This includes using restraint when tempted to lecture about how you did everything.

I regularly get letters from distraught grandmas who are banned from seeing their grandchild. This is a terrible consequence for everyone involved—the child, the parent, and the grandparent. We need generational relationships, and God intended them to be a source of security and support. So how can we navigate this season of life with grace?

The earliest accounts in the Bible and history reflect the concept of generational relationships between parents, children, and grandparents. Proverbs 17:6 says, "Children's children are a crown to the aged, and parents are the pride of their children." Sometimes young parents view the things that their parents did wrong with such disdain and resolve to "do it different" that they can fail to see the tremendous vintage value in having family support systems, welcoming advice on taking care of an infant and lifelong support parenting a child. Not to mention that godly grandparents can be the best babysitters to trust! It is a beautiful discovery from all perspectives if we can learn to work together with love and respect.

So much in life just comes back to the Golden Rule: "Do unto others as you would have them do unto you." If parents and grandparents honor and respect one another, this is a much easier task to accomplish. We should be just as committed to support our adult children as they raise their children "in the nurture and the admonition of the Lord" as we were ours, but our role *is* different. We do not have the final say or responsibility and must respect our children's decisions. We can lovingly share our thoughts in a respectful manner, but not in front of the child. Share your concern or observation gingerly and then leave the seed in their heart to take root. Pray first, carefully sow it, leave it alone, and pray some more. That's it.

Family division can result if grandparents disrespect the parents by making little remarks in an effort to win the grandchild's allegiance. "Grandma will let you have it, even if daddy won't!" This is unacceptable behavior. It's not a competition for the child's heart, rather a common goal of doing what is best for the child's development. If you as a parent find yourself in this situation with a grandparent, you must prayerfully and lovingly address your parents with the utmost honor for their position and not in front of the child. The person best suited to do this is usually the adult son or daughter of the grandparent. Parents naturally have a tendency to blame the in-law and vice versa, so they will likely be much more understanding and forgiving if their own child talks about delicate issues. It also alleviates a "he said, she said" divisiveness. This may not be the situation in every in-law relationship, but be wise.

Sometimes the in-laws will corner the daughter-in-law to "work on her" when they don't want to deal directly with their son. This triangulation quickly makes the daughter-in-law the troublemaker, stuck in the middle trying to represent herself and her husband and what was said between them while being drawn into a disagreement. If this happens to you, gently share with them it would be best to speak to their son, since you are honoring *his* family leadership. Then kindly remove yourself from the discussion or change the subject with respect and civility but firmness that will not allow manipulation by the grandparent.

> As grandparents, you must respect the choices of your adult children or you may find yourself ostracized from your adorable grandchild.

Remember: Grandparents are learning the new arrangement, too, so give them some grace, just not the authority to take over. If you suppress frustrations instead of communicating, it could result in an unfortunate eruption that damages relationships between the families. There are families that have lost wonderful years of fulfilling exchanges because of hurt feelings and bitterness. It's not worth it. We've all had to traverse through some family misunderstandings. It happens in every generation.

One of our family rules was that our children (ages 3–9 at the time) could not see any movie other than G-rated or an occasional PG if we previewed it first. Gary's parents felt we were being too strict. We left our three children (then) with them for an evening out, reminding them about our guidelines. While we were in the middle of dinner, I suddenly had a sick feeling that something was wrong with the children. I encouraged Gary we must go back. As we walked into the house, our three-year-old came screaming through the foyer crying at the top of his lungs. They were showing the children a PG-13 movie, a scary scene had just occurred, and our son was horrified.

I did not feel comfortable leaving our children unaccompanied with them again for many years. It was sad to me, because I wanted to have that kind of trust relationship, but their choices hurt our ability to trust. However, even though I felt like it, I did not react in a manner that would destroy our future relationship. I quietly packed the kids up and Gary handled the situation. We continued to love Grandma and Grandpa and make sure we spent time together. We just didn't leave our children in their care alone until the kids were older and better able to discern how to handle discrepancies.

The beautiful thing that happened as the years rolled by was that our family was able to demonstrate our love and keep a relationship that resulted in salvation to Gary's father. They were always wonderful people, but we had differing standards because of our beliefs about training a child's heart, and we had to protect our children from harm.

As parents, you must navigate these tense moments with love but not compromise. As grandparents, you must respect the choices of your adult children or you may find yourself ostracized from your adorable grandchild. I can think of few things sadder than missing out on this time. If you've already made mistakes here, take responsibility and sincerely apologize. Pray for an opportunity that you can once again be a part of their life. Isaiah 46:4–5 promises, "Even to your old age and gray hairs I am he, I am he who will sustain you. I have made you and I will carry you; I will sustain you and I will rescue you."

Sometimes you must agree to disagree agreeably. As a grandparent, if you're trying to bring a godly standard to your grandchild against the parents' wishes, do it slowly with prayer and with careful respect of the parents. You can catch more bees with honey than vinegar, the saying goes. Babysit for them and be a source of encouragement and never defy their requests even if you feel they are unnecessary (unless illegal or unethical). Psalm 103:17 says, "But from everlasting to everlasting the LORD's love is with those who fear him, and his righteousness with their children's children."

Prayer and serving *in love* can give you a platform of influence at the right time. Be patient and wait for it. The time will inevitably come when they will want your counsel or advice, but if you're pushy, condescending, and critical of their parenting, you will have an adverse impact on this opportunity. It could result in a divisive family breakdown. Don't risk it! It's not worth it to make your point.

Embrace Your New Role

So what areas can a grandparent or family member impact? Remember the television show *The Waltons*, with grandparents living under the roof with the family? The grandfather took the boys fishing, taught them life skills, and had time to offer a listening ear when dad was busy at work. Grandma helped make the family dinner, and the entire family was home every Sunday for dinner after church. This may work better on television than in real life, but certainly family gatherings can help accomplish this even if living under the same roof may prove to be a bad idea.

Grandparents can teach skills, help with homework, purchase a gift, make a craft, or share a hobby. They can share family history, showing pictures of their parents when they were small and other family members. This gives children a sense of identity and security. Often they have time to do things that busy parents may not. They can encourage good behavior and reinforce obedience to parents. They can teach manners and respect with a gentle accepting heart of love. They can cook family meals and provide a place for fun and parties.

I was thrilled when Gary's father offered to pay for our girls' dance lessons for a year as a Christmas gift. Consider furthering your grandchildren's education with classes or zoo passes or family fun packages if you're in a financial situation to do so (and Mom and Dad approve).

Recapture the vintage picture of gathering weekly to reconnect today. I know a large multigenerational family that has had an open pizza party every Friday evening for over twenty years. It's available to them, and family members regularly show up! Everyone doesn't always come, but more often than not they do. It's aided their family to weather some storms and bring them back home in hard times.

As grandparents, it's hard to recognize that getting the entire crew together consistently may not be possible. There is something in every parent that wants it to be like it used to be, to get all the kids together and relive the "good ole days." It may be harder to manage in today's transient, disconnected world. Use video messaging, social media, and creative gifts and trips to reconnect the family as much as possible, but realize it will not be the same as it was raising your family, and that's fine. Embrace the new vintage family and make the most of it by being positive and grateful for what you have and the new memories you can make with your grandchildren, even if it's reading a book over Skype or Facetime.

One grandma shared with me that she babysits over Skype almost every Friday night, talking, reading, and entertaining her grandchild, both living across the country from one another while the mom does her company bookwork in the adjoin-

> Grandparents who are wise can use this as a wonderful life-changing adventure with their grandchildren and can be a second voice to confirm what their mom and dad train and model.

ing room. She decided to fly in one Friday and surprise her grandchild in person for their Friday night date (with Mom's knowledge). The small child was ecstatic, and later told her grandma she didn't have to go back in the box again!

Another grandma I spoke with hosts a Grandma Camp every summer at her home. She makes elaborate plans for crafts, games, field trips, and a sleepover in a tent in the backyard. She themes her camps using medieval castles, knights, princesses, and dragons. I'm looking forward to hosting a "Grand-mama Camp" myself from her inspiration as soon as my grandbabies are old enough! I've had an occasional overnight experience, and it was great fun! Have fun and refuse to get old! It's a choice. "They will still bear fruit in old age, they will stay fresh and green" (Psalm 92:14).

Conversely, I've seen couples whose parents want almost no involvement with their grandchildren and do not accept the joy of being a grandparent. They see it as, "I raised my kids. I am not ready to be a grandparent." It *is* an adjustment to age, and sometimes these grandparents see grandchildren as a reminder. If that's your parents, give them some time to make the mental maneuver; try to be as positive as you can, and let them experience your child in small doses at their pace. Most will come around when they have an encounter of love.

I think it's safe to say that all grandparents have to adjust to grandchildren, especially after being empty nesters. All children are different and have their own unique personalities and gifts. Don't compare them; just embrace their individuality. Our grandson Dawson is like a little tank going full speed, sometimes crashing into things, falling, laughing, and getting back up to do it again. My husband can barely watch, fearing the little guy will get hurt. He turned to me and said, "How did we raise five kids?" Our big-brown-eyed little Cady is such a nurturer, holding a dolly and blanket cuddled to her chest since six months old. She always finds the baby doll and holds it as a mommy would a baby.

Ivory at two is a country cutie and loves to catch and hold frogs of all sizes, even huge bullfrogs. She giggles in delight and simply loves them! I have to act as though I'm not terrified. I bought her a stuffed animal frog from Cracker Barrel (the grandparents' store), and when I told her it was a frog, she looked at me as though I was from Mars and proceeded to find a real frog and show it to me.

One evening I kept Journey who had just turned three and could easily double as Shirley Temple! Head full of brown curls, she skipped and danced around my living room singing at the top of her lungs to "Just a Spoon Full of Sugar" as together we experienced Mary Poppins. I had a flashback, remembering the sheer delight I had seeing the same movie the first time at the theater as a little girl.

Parenting requires almost everything of a person, so having an occasional break can be a lifesaver. Grandparents who are wise can use this as a wonderful life-changing adventure with their grandchildren and can be a second voice to confirm what their mom and dad train and model. A second voice unified around the same cause, training the next generation for the purpose of God in their life. Psalm 145:4 reminds us, "One generation commends your works to another; they tell of your mighty acts."

Have you had strong family support while raising your children? Has that made it easier or harder?

....

....

....

....

....

....

What is your vision for when you are a grandparent? Or if you already are a grandparent, what kind of grandparent do you aim to be?

....

....

....

....

....

....

What can you take from this chapter and apply to your life?

....

....

....

....

....

....

....

Keep It Classy

Good manners and kindness are always in fashion. Manners have always been an important communication tool and consideration for others. Training your children how to treat others with respect and to mind their manners is certainly a vintage family value that has an important place in today's modern world.

For starters, employ these manners:

Make sure you say: "Please," "Thank you," and "You're welcome."

Say: "Excuse me," when you need to excuse yourself from a situation or leave, or pass someone or accidentally bump another person.

When you make a mistake, offer a genuine apology. "I'm sorry."

Say and do things in a pleasant way even when you must communicate something you cannot do that another wishes. "I am sorry I will not be able to attend the dinner."

Cover your mouth when you sneeze or cough.

Offer your name when you answer the phone residence: "Hello, this is (name). May I help you?"

Share a cheerful greeting and inquire of others' welfare: "Hello, how are you today?"

Give the person speaking your full attention in private or public settings and make good eye contact.

Acknowledge gifts with a thank you, either in card, call, or other written acknowledgment.

There were lots of laughs during this family photo shoot, Mother's Day 2014!

There's Still Hope

GROWN-UP KIDS
MAKE MISTAKES

"Children need love, especially when they don't deserve it."

HAROLD HULBERT

I used to have the false illusion that once your children grew up, the huge feeling of responsibility would no longer be there, but truthfully, it increases. But don't let that be a source of discouragement! The reality is that God didn't create us to ever stop investing in our family and others. Our children are in young adulthood, and although they are navigating very well, it's challenging to live life in any generation. The world of grown-ups—buying houses, paying bills, having babies, raising children, taking care of health insurance, taxes, employment, relationships, marriage, and all the responsibilities of life—can be overwhelming to any adult. Young people need our prayers and encouragement!

The role of a parent must change, however, or we create dysfunction in their lives. When they become adults, they are not under our authority any longer, and we must readjust our approach and relationship. You won't always agree with their decisions or choices, and that's all right, but you must give them independence and respect.

I spoke to a mother who constantly worried over her adult son, reminding him about past mistakes and warning about future ones, which caused him to nearly shut her out of his life completely. She treated him like a little boy, making him feel disrespected and like he was already doomed to fail even though he was trying to move in the right direction. She finally realized she was doing the exact thing to her son that her mother had done to her. I encouraged her to apologize for getting into his personal business and to say positive things about him while he was in this valley. "I believe in you. I respect you as a man, and I know you will make the right decisions." Then get out of the way and pray! She took my advice and happily reported they were planning a long awaited visit and were on speaking terms again.

We all probably have had someone in our life who played this nagging role. Can you remember how it felt to be disrespected by someone with comments that placed guilt or fear on you? How did you respond? We usually run the other way or submit to their controlling words outwardly, but inwardly build incredible resentment that can turn to bitterness and estrangement over time.

We all need to know we are loved and accepted as well as forgiven for any past mistakes. People that "guilt" us into doing what they want quickly become a person we inadvertently or intentionally choose to avoid. If your first comment to your adult child's phone call is, "You never call me," that's manipulative, and you aren't likely to get more calls, and if you do, they will be out of obligation, not out of relationship. Build a bridge by being positive, grateful, and let them talk about what they want. If you start badgering them with an interrogation, they won't call or visit again very soon or often.

I know how hard it is to release our adult children to God, but we must. Trying to fix their mistakes and "do" for them what they must do for themselves creates a dysfunction and codependency. Look at the epidemic of adult young men who have not accepted responsibility for any of their choices because often their parents have prolonged their childhood by letting them remain little boys at home playing video games instead of developing their futures. You cannot do for someone what they need to do, or they will never learn the consequences of their decisions. Handing your children off to God is important; learning to depend on God and His direction for their life is, too.

You are in a new season in your life's journey that God wants to develop as well. The forties and fifties are a time to train and teach others what you've learned in life, yet that wisdom must be sought out; where there is no honor, you can teach nothing.

Recently on a trip to Japan, I saw the positive impact of honor instilled in young people from an early age. As a result, young people seek their parents' wisdom and respect and honor elders' advice. A young person gains a great advantage in life to learn from the mistakes of someone older and wiser. This is a vintage value that has eroded badly in our culture, and we're paying a price for it.

Honor and respect are vintage values young parents should nurture in their children. Start it by your example of how you show honor to your parents, to those who have served in our nation's military, and to those who serve as police officers, firefighters, ministers, coaches, and teachers. These instill much-needed good manners.

Navigating the release of adult children is a process that can involve great joy as well as some bumps along the road. We all make some mistakes starting out. I encourage you not to overreact to the bumps of adolescence or young adulthood choices.

Hopefully you started letting them make some quality decisions in the teen years, so your young adult children are already experienced. I'm not talking about smoking pot or premarital sex; I'm talking about mixing freedom with responsibility. If you did it all for them and shielded them from any repercussions of bad decisions, they will have to learn a few things the harder way now. Pray for them every day and offer your counsel without judgment where they will receive it, always with encouragement and the reassurance that you believe in them and God at work in their lives. Stop paying for their mistakes or it will prolong them growing up and taking responsibility.

> Handing your children off to God is important; learning to depend on God and His direction for their life is, too.

If your child is not serving God, remember that He sees them and He is working on their heart as a result of your prayers. "The LORD is close to the brokenhearted and saves those who are crushed in spirit" (Psalm 34:18). Pray their eyes be open to God's ways and their heart be softened to hear His voice and obey Him. Then, let go, even if you have to go through this process every day.

If you haven't already done so, start looking for ways to build your personal life and devote your time to those who need and desire what you have to offer. Why sit at home fretting over your children and accomplish nothing else in the process? You can't add one minute to your life by worrying, but you can throw your life away micromanaging your children. You have wisdom and gifts others need.

You may also have other children who have not turned away from you who are being neglected while you chase after one who has. This can feel like rejection to them. Let the joy of the

Lord be your strength. If your life is positive and attractive, it offers security and stability to all your family.

Some parents of adult children turn away from God when their children rebel. If you faint in the day of adversity, your strength is small (Proverbs 24:10). If you've let the bumpy road of life cause *you* to stray, get back where you need to be in God's household, so when your child returns, he or she will know you will already be there waiting.

Forgiveness and Love

I love the story of the prodigal son in Luke 15, but it is really the story of a loving father. The son demanded his inheritance from his father, which in essence was saying, "I don't respect you, and I wish you were dead. Give me what I want." He was selfish and had no regard for his father or family. After he left home and squandered the inheritance on riotous living and wrong relationships, notice the father did not chase after him, but continued about his business and responsibilities with the other son who remained at home.

Eventually the prodigal had nothing left and hit bottom, but he remembered the goodness of his father and decided to go home. What if his father had decided to give up life because his son hurt him? What if the father had become bitter and forbade the son to ever return? What if his father had kept sending him more money to bail him out of situations? Would the prodigal have ever come home?

"So he got up and went to his father. *But while he was still a long way off,* his father saw him and was filled with compassion for him; he ran to his son, threw his arms around him and kissed him" (Luke 15:20). Isn't that amazing? The father's love was greater than the sin of his son. He never gave up believing for his son's return. The fathered covered the son's past with a robe of his own righteousness, gave him the family ring, sandals, and a great party. He didn't bring up the past, but rather he saw his son's future. This is the kind of encouragement we all need when we've blown it.

We know that the father represents God, but this beautiful love story of our God also exemplifies how a father or mother handles those who are grown adults and make decisions to depart from truth. God shows His unconditional love even when His children aren't where they need to be, and that is what we can do as parents as well.

Stop thinking of and rehearsing the pain they've caused you. Refuse bitterness and forgive them, but also let go and release *them* to make the decision to turn back to God. You should pray, and prayer is very effective, but you can't decide for them. If you try, you're an easy target for manipulation, only delaying their need for real change. Many young adults manipulate their "praying mamas" for money and anything else they can get from them. Be wise! This can also come between a husband and wife, dividing their marriage over disagreements dealing with the wayward child. Stay united and decide together how you will handle situations. A united position will stop the enemy from entering your marriage and creating more havoc.

I've prayed with women in their later years who are broke and about to be evicted because they have given all they have on wayward kids, and it hasn't worked. It's only delayed the inevitable. In 1 Corinthians 5:5, the apostle Paul said, "I have decided to hand this man over to Satan for the destruction of the flesh, so that his spirit may be saved on the day of the Lord." Sometimes sin must run its course that they may repent and be saved. As difficult as it sounds, when sin brought the prodigal son to the bottom, *he* decided to return and on the father's terms, not his own selfish demands. He came home to be a servant, to make restitution, to do his part, not expecting the rights or privileges he had thrown away so carelessly. Yet the father, seeing his brokenness, restored him to being a son, not regarding or reminding him of his failure.

As a parent, live the life He destined you to live. Let your children see your joy, your peace, your provision, and your steadfastness in God. Instead of you grieving and throwing your life away because they have chosen to depart, hold steadfast to the Father's house and love. When they truly return, you will have a robe and ring to offer in love.

As much as we love our children, our love for God must be more important than any human relationship (Matthew 10:37). This doesn't mean we turn against children who have gone wayward, but we do choose Jesus and stay in the Father's house while we pray for them to come to their senses, just as the prodigal son eventually did. Staying in the Father's love is the only way you will be able to offer your child real love with the right perspective.

When I played basketball, I learned that the best defense is a good offense. Let your offense be that you are going to be all God says, and in faith serve Him and your purpose in Christ, even if someone you love chooses not to. Your best opportunity to see their turnaround will come if you continue in God's promises and honor Him as an example to your family. You will find courage, strength, and answers in Father's house.

Don't be harsh, critical, or judge them. Beware of pushing religious rules that often have little to do with biblical truths, which is why they stay away! Religion is not the same as God's love. Negative words aren't words of faith. Instead, let God's love help you believe the best in faith for your child. It will eventually touch their heart. Faith is calling those things that do not exist as though they did (Romans 4:17).

God saw you and me when we were dead in our sins and sent His Son to die for us before we said yes. That's how much He believed we would eventually make the right choice.

One daughter had shut her mother out of her life. She considered her parents' faith as antiquated and unnecessary, thinking her education and success had replaced her need for God. Initially, these parents were critical and embarrassed by their daughter's behavior. But as her mother started to love her unconditionally, offering to serve her in helpful and practical ways (without preaching a word), she felt their love, not necessarily acceptance of all the choices she made, but of her as a person. Healing and forgiveness began to flow and restore the relationship. She began to open her heart and life back up to her parents.

> As much as we love our children, our love for God must be more important than any human relationship (Matthew 10:37).

Another family had a daughter who rebelled, moved away, and was living in a lesbian relationship. They were heartbroken. One Sunday I prayed with them for this confused young woman. I felt led to pray that the soul ties and control would be broken in the relationship, and their beautiful daughter would return home to them and Jesus. She called them the next day and asked to come home. The relationship was over, and she wanted to return to her family and God.

Sometimes the journey back home takes longer than parents' hope for, but if home is an inviting place of love and steadfastness in Christ, it's hard to resist. Forgiveness and love are vintage values that go back as far as the beginning of creation.

Do you believe that you are called to be a parent? Why or why not?

....

....

....

....

....

What does the call and charge of being a parent mean to you?

....

....

....

....

....

....

Have you renounced and chosen to break with wrong beliefs and past sins so that you do not pass them on to your children?

....

....

....

....

....

....

What can you take away from this book and apply to your everyday life?

....

....

....

....

....

....

We know how to have fun together!

Admiring the remarkable architecture of Paris and visiting places we had taught the kids about in their school lessons. (Back left to right: Tim, Tom, and Gary. Front: Kirsten, Drenda, Amy, and Polly.)

"Children's children are a crown to the aged..." (Proverbs 17:6). We're so blessed by our grandbabies! (Gary holding Dawson, Drenda holding Cadence, Ivory and Journey, seated.)

CONCLUSION

Provide the Finishing Touch

After reading the wonderful monographs of childhood from my children, I realize what mattered most to them is relationship. It's easy to get caught up in the work of building a family and miss out on the relationships in building a family. Sometimes we think that what we're doing is the most important task—cleaning house, doing laundry, washing cars, and working, working, working. And while all these things are important, Jesus said it best when addressing Mary and Martha.

"'Martha, Martha,' the Lord answered, 'you are worried and upset about many things, but few things are needed—or indeed only one. Mary has chosen what is better, and it will not be taken away from her'" (Luke 10:42).

We often get caught up with the hustle and bustle of keeping house and maintaining everything, but we forget what is really important. Our children don't remember washed cars! They remember the joys of laughter, times together, and the relationship of knowing Jesus through our relationship with them.

Many times I was laboring while our beautiful children were jumping on the trampoline with their dad or hearing one of his famous stories. And while I did make things fun and enjoy great times with my children, I still wish I would have made more time for the simple joys, the vintage pleasures of rolling on the floor laughing or playing outside. Like Martha, I reasoned that someone had to do the work. It's easy to reason that tomorrow we will have more time with our family, but unless you make it a priority today, that day never comes. Don't get caught up in the duties and lose the beauty of simple relationship. Are you building a relationship with your family and with the Creator of family? That's what will be remembered in the end. It's not *things* that children need more of; it's *time*.

We have to take account for how we spend our time on the earth. Personal responsibility is the first movement toward change and reconstruction. Do it for yourself and for those you love. Many have chosen to let the government or institutions take responsibility for their lives, their children, their finances and choices. The problem is, when you give away personal responsibility, you also let go of the freedom you had to make a life for yourself. Life becomes robotic and hopeless, because others become our source instead of God.

As we reach the end of our journey, I want to give you the opportunity to commemorate your family and to commit to yourself that you will restyle your family using timeless ways that hearken back to a vintage system—God's system. I encourage you to commit to making a change in your family, listen to God's direction, and move forward with the right foundation.

Parenting is a great calling. God called you to your family, and He has given you the grace to do it. My desire is that you leave this book with a renewed vision for your family and recapture the love and simplicity of days gone by . . . more of what matters.

We have to weather the storms and fight for our families. We have to fight for the time-tested family model and revitalize honor toward the family system. There's an attack on families, children, and unborn babies, and it's our job to lead the movement to save them. The best defense is a great offense—a family that shines in a dark place. We can pray that the culture will turn back to the vintage model and realign themselves with their origin and purpose from God's Word, but we have our part to play, and it starts with personal revival.

You have the baton. Generations have come before us and may come after us, but right now, it's your turn. Your story is being written in history. The stories that your grandkids are going to tell about you are being walked out right now. The victories that your kids are going to see are happening right now. You may have made mistakes, but it's not too late to make a change in your situation—to be refashioned and repurposed and reclaim the promises of God for your home. It takes courage, but the moment you step up, God is going to meet you at the doorway to home.

Live by faith—that is the most exciting way to live!

If you have anything in your life that is keeping you apart from your Father, your Creator, something more important than God, you need to reestablish your foundation. Things in moderation are good, but God should be the clear center of your family. And sometimes it's just that you're letting the cares of life choke God and His design out. That doesn't work. Only God as the center works.

Maybe today you're struggling in your marriage, or you're struggling as a single parent—God's grace is sufficient for you. God is more than enough. Stay committed and let Him show you there's a way out of the pain without running away. There's a way to victory. There's a way to healing. There's a way right now if you choose forgiveness. Run to God; He has the answers for your life.

I encourage you to speak this prayer out loud and make a commitment in your heart. If you want to humble yourself before your Father God to show you and teach you, open your heart and take a step of faith. God will act.

> *Lord, I thank You for healing in my family, my marriage, and in myself. I dedicate my family to You, God. Please give me direction on disconnects in my family and things I need to change. I thank You for the grace to make the changes I need to make, and the wisdom to know how.*
>
> *God, give me wisdom to help fight for families and marriages all around the world. I thank You for healing in the culture.*
>
> *I commit my heart to doing this Your way. I am going to fight for my family with Your Word and Your principles, and I know You will meet me there and give me the ability to overcome. Thank You for the great calling You've given me to be a parent.*
>
> *In Jesus' name, Amen!*

I encourage you to commemorate each of your family members by writing five qualities you admire in them and sharing them with your family. Make a written commitment to yourself that proclaims the changes you would like to implement, the parenting insecurities you're leaving behind, and the end result for which you're aiming. Sign it at the bottom and keep it somewhere safe to remind you of the commitment you've made to your family.

❖ ENDNOTES ❖

1 Neil Shah, "Unmarried with Children," *The Wall Street Journal*, March 11, 2015.

2 http://www.jacksonkatz.com/PDF/ChildrenMedia.pdf

3 http://metro.co.uk/2013/10/09/gta-5-breaks-seven-guin-ness-world-records-as-global-addiction-continues-4139807/

4 http://internet-filter-review.toptenreviews.com/internet-pornography-statistics.html

5 http://www.letsgo.org/wp-content/uploads/3-S-2-Facts-and-Figures-About-Our-TV-Habit-Tab-1-DOUBLE-SIDED.pdf

6 Ibid.

7 Ibid.

8 Kaiser Family Foundation

9 http://home.snu.edu/~hculbert/ages.htm

10 see Home School Legal Defense, www.hslda.org

11 http://www.focusonthefamily.com/marriage/gods-design-for-marriage/marriage-gods-idea/reflecting-our-relation-ship-with-god

For more tips, resources, and downloads visit

THE *Vintage* FAMILY.ORG / bonus